SEEING
CAPITOL REEF
NATIONAL PARK
A Guide to the roads
and trails

by
Ward J. Roylance

Wasatch Publishers, Inc.
1979

**To
Gloria**

**Book design
and artwork by
L. Goff Dowding**

© Copyright 1979
Wasatch Publishers, Inc.
4647 Idlewild Road
Salt Lake City, Utah 84117
All rights reserved
ISBN 0-915272-22-9
LCN 79-63770

Front cover, **Golden Throne,** *NPS photo.*
Back cover, **Lower South Desert,** *Fran Barnes photo.*

CONTENTS

Acknowledgments

Many people deserve credit for whatever is good in this book. Gloria, my dear wife, gave constant inspiration. Without the encouragement of Mel Davis, publisher, and Fran Barnes there would be no book. I hope their trust is justified.

Lurt and Alice Knee opened new Capitol Reef vistas for me in years gone by. Local flavor, advice and tales of the past came from Dewey and Nell Gifford, Riley and Erma Osborn, Don Pace, Cass Mulford, Evangeline Tappan Godby, and other "old-timers." Special boosters include Roselyn and Don Phillips, Frank and Lela Sweeney.

I must not fail to mention Charles Kelly, first superintendent of Capitol Reef National Monument, whom I knew in life and whose legacy of research and writing was indispensable for this work.

Numerous published and manuscript sources were consulted. I regret they cannot be listed, but my appreciation to their authors is nonetheless heartfelt.

Without the advice and assistance of park personnel this book would lack much of its value as a guide. Bob Reynolds, Chief Park Interpreter, gave generous support in providing research materials and photographs; he also provided valuable suggestions and corrected errors. Rangers Bill Hauze and Tom Townley taught me much about their districts, animated me with their enthusiasm, and made corrections and suggestions for this work.

I wish to emphasize that inaccuracies are my own. Reader comments will be most sincerely appreciated.

Ward J. Roylance

Torrey, Utah 84775

Foreword

Trying to describe Capitol Reef National Park is a humbling experience. Words are too inadequate, emotions too jumbled.

I have known Capitol Reef for more than 30 years. During that time, until recently, it was not quite my favorite place. Now it is. As with any acquired taste, it grows on you. You must savor it, taste and retaste, become intimately familiar with it. Its charms are subtle; but when finally they have captivated you, there is no release.

Capitol Reef has so many nuances of personality that the casual visitor becomes aware of only a few at any one time. True, its physical grandeur and the radiance of its coloring are overwhelming at first glance. The impact of these never lessens. And the chaotic setting of bare rocks, carved in fascinating shapes and nestled beneath brooding plateaus and alpine peaks, is a deep emotional experience in itself.

In most of life's situations, superficial impressions must suffice. This would have been the case for Gloria and me, with respect to Capitol Reef, if we had not decided, several years ago, to make our home near the Reef in Torrey. Since then, far from breeding contempt or boredom, familiarity brings ever growing awe at the wonder of the park and its surroundings. The land is more incredibly beautiful every day. At times its grandeur makes us weak. It is all so *unbelievable!*

I truly hope that this book will help the reader to gain expanded awareness of what the park offers in the way of beauty and adventure. If, in addition, the book plants a seed of desire to return again and again, to explore and meditate and "commune," then I will be overjoyed.

CAPITOL REEF
an introduction to the Park . . .

CAPITOL REEF
an introduction to the Park

As the essence of a mystic experience — even a taste or smell — cannot be conveyed in words, so it is with Capitol Reef National Park. Its uniqueness defies language.

Geologically the Waterpocket Fold, foundation of the park, is not too unusual in such basic attributes as its rock layers (which are common throughout much of the Colorado Plateau), or its numberless erosional forms (which have general counterparts elsewhere), or its dramatic monoclinal structure (other picturesque monoclines are in the vicinity). Even the varied colors of its rocks, while superlative, can be found in other parts of the Four Corners region.

No, the uniqueness of Capitol Reef National Park lies not merely in its basic geological constitutents, however remarkable they might be. The secret of its sublimity is in the blending, the polishing, the finishing.

Any work of art requires raw materials. What transforms materials into art is some creative force, be it human genius or natural impulse, as well as a fortuitous combination of those materials.

In the case of Capitol Reef the creative impulse (erosion) has combined with ideal materials to create a masterpiece of *natural esthetics.*

Esthetics: *pertaining to beauty or the beautiful.* Perhaps esthetics is the key concept in evaluating the park. Its beauty is different from that of any other place. The park stands in an esthetic class by itself, setting its own distinctive standard of beauty. There is nothing else like it.

At Capitol Reef nature has taken ordinary raw materials (rocks), painted in a spectrum of rainbow hues, and shaped them into a work of amazing erosional intricacy. Maze, tangle and labyrinth are descriptive terms that are eminently suitable here. So are adjectives such as strange, marvelous, exquisite, harmonious, majestic — the list could go on without exaggeration.

And what to call the park's natural forms? The English language is hardly adequate to describe some of them.

Canyons? Yes, but not merely "canyons." In Capitol Reef they are chasms...gorges...gulches...slots...natural phenomena that Webster never dreamed of.

Buttes? Yes, but in Capitol Reef a "butte" is likely to be a rounded, swelling, doming, swirling object of esthetic perfection. The angular butte named by Spanish explorers bears little resemblance to the splended butte-forms of Capitol Reef.

Cliffs? Yes, hundreds of miles of them. But in Capitol Reef they are not merely "cliffs." Here they have a delightful personality all their own, the result of rainbow coloring and wonderful erosional designs.

All of this color, erosional intricacy and uniqueness of personality make Capitol Reef a park for connoisseurs. There is no end to esthetic discovery. Every change in perspective reveals new forms and relationships. Clouds...sunlight...moonlight...time of day... rain...snow: every nuance of lighting and contrast creates new colors, shapes, spatial dimensions. The possibilities for visual experience seem boundless here.

And so, this book itself can be but an introduction — and an invitation to begin your own voyage of discovery at Capitol Reef.

Visitor Center and The Castle   *NPS photo*

HISTORICAL BACKGROUND

Fremont storage granary *NPS photo*

Typical Fremont crops *NPS photo*

Fremont baskets *NPS photo*

HISTORICAL BACKGROUND

THE INDIANS

The Fremont Culture

The striking rock art (also called rock writing) on the cliff east of the Visitor Center, and in Capitol Gorge, was created by Indians who lived in the park area more than 700 years ago.

These prehistoric people belonged to what is now called the Fremont culture. They were contemporaries of the better known Anasazi cliff dwellers of Mesa Verde and other pueblos of the Four Corners area, though some of their cultural traits differed to a degree — almost as America's rural cultures of today differ in certain aspects from urban cultures.

Within the park boundaries, not much remains of the Fremont culture other than pictographs and petroglyphs on cliff faces and boulders, and a few granaries here and there in rock niches. White settlers discovered the most important Fremont dwelling sites, and collected the most significant cultural materials, years before scientific investigators arrived.

The Fremont people did not build sturdy masonry structures, as did contemporary Indians to the south and east. They preferred less durable pit houses built of rock, adobe and wood, often located on knolls, ridges or terraces that overlooked their farm plots. These houses long since washed away, or they collapsed, leaving only the foundation stones. Even when caves were utilized — and suitable caves are scarce in the park area — structures were comparatively rude and non-durable. The result is that archeologists do not have an abundance of evidence from which to form a picture of the Fremont culture; and much of the evidence they do have comes from sites outside the present-day park.

There was no systematic, comprehensive survey by scientists until the late 1920's, when specialists from Peabody Museum surveyed

13

and excavated numerous sites in the Waterpocket Fold, the Torrey-Grover area, Boulder, and along the east slope of Boulder Mountain.

From this survey came the name Fremont Culture, which has been used ever since to identify a common culture that is now known to have existed over a vast area of 20,000 square miles, extending from central Utah to western Colorado, and from the Uinta Mountains southward to the San Juan and Escalante rivers.

In more recent years it has been found that the culture's areas of densest population actually were north of Capitol Reef, in Castle Valley (Emery County) and Nine-Mile Canyon. However, it is likely that the entire Fremont population never totaled more than a few thousand.

How did the Fremont people live? They were hunters, gatherers and farmers. They hunted mountain sheep and rabbit, deer, elk, buffalo, antelope, prairie dog, gopher and ground squirrel; also bear, beaver and coyote. They fished. They gathered pinyon pine nuts, bulbs and sunflower seeds.

The Fremonts grew maize (corn), beans and squash. These were often stored in rock and adobe granaries, still to be seen in several places throughout the park.

Their weapons were the bow and arrow, and to some extent the atlal. To trap small animals they used snares and nets. Pointed sticks were used for digging; also, perhaps, shovels and hoes. Irrigation ditches carried water to their fields, and traces of these ditches were still visible when whites arrived.

The Fremonts differed from the Anasazi pueblo peoples of their time in several noteworthy respects: They did not build substantial buildings...They wore fur moccasins instead of sandals and depended to a greater extent on hunting (probably in both cases because of a colder climate)...They did not use cotton or raise domesticated turkeys...They did not develop the ceremonial kiva. And though their pottery was comparatively plain, their rock art ranks among the finest in North America; also, some of their clay figurines are remarkable.

The Fremonts were fond of ornamentation. This is apparent from their rock art (rock writing), which depicts necklaces and breast pendants, and what appear to be horned headdresses. Jewelry has been found, some of it elaborate.

Fremont rock art in the Fruita-Torrey-Grover area is considered to be outstanding. Other examples are found throughout the Canyonlands region and Uinta area. Some rank among the choicest treasures of primitive art, including Fremont panels in Dry Fork Canyon and Horseshoe Canyon.

Where did the Fremont Indians come from? Where did they go?

The Anasazi pueblo cultures south of the Fremont area are known to have developed for more than a thousand years, from before the time of Christ. The Fremonts, on the other hand, seem not to have arrived in their cultural area until about 950 A.D. Their origin is

Post-Fremont rock art *Fran Barnes photo*

uncertain, but there are close similarities to the Anasazi culture of southern Utah known as the Virgin culture. They also resembled the Sevier Puebloid culture, which flourished to the west.

Nobody knows with certainty why their stable farming culture died and where the people went. But there is reason to believe that the same drouth which drove the Anasazi from their settlements was responsible for demise of the Fremont culture around 1200 A.D.— only 250 years or so from its blossoming. One hypothesis which seems to have support is that the Fremont people remained in the area, and their descendants are the Utes and Southern Paiutes of historic times—hunters and gatherers who, in places, also cultivated crops.

Indians of Historic Times

When the Catholic padres Dominguez and Escalante passed through Utah in 1776, as the first whites to enter the state, they were guided by Ute Indians—and they found a community of Utes at Utah Lake. Utes and Paiutes occupied most of mountain and plateau Utah.

White explorers and pioneers of the Fremont River valleys, including the Fish Lake country, encountered Paiute Indians who eked out a perilous existence by fishing, hunting and gathering. Both races lived in proximity for several decades, until finally the Indians settled in Grass Valley or moved elsewhere. It was customary, when the whites arrived, for the local Indians to reside at Fish Lake during warmer months, then migrate into the lower deserts and canyons east of Capitol Reef in winter. Probably this was an age-old custom.

The Whites

The Capitol Reef area is a rugged, arid land having few economic advantages that might have attracted non-Indians before they actually arrived at a relatively late date. It remained *terra incognita* longer, almost, than any other part of Utah except the far southeast. Serious exploration and first colonization did not come until the 1870's, and settlement continued through the 1880's.

Exploration

There is no written record that white men saw the Capitol Reef area before 1866, when a party of Mormon militia from St. George, in pursuit of marauding Indians, looked eastward from Boulder Mountain. It is probable, however, that fur trappers and New Mexicans were in the region before that.

The main Spanish Trail between New Mexico and southern California crossed the Fish Lake Plateau, about 40 miles west of Fruita. Evidence indicates that a branch of this, used during winter months, passed across the Henry Mountains and Waterpocket Fold.

In the winter of 1853-54 a group of explorers led by John Charles Fremont passed through the general area. Their exact route is unclear, but it is likely they followed the Spanish route across the Fish Lake highlands. However that may be, Fremont's name later was applied to the first Mormon settlement in Wayne County, and to the area's major stream.

Major John W. Powell made his first epic journey down the Green and Colorado rivers in 1869, following this with a second, more scientific river survey in 1871. During the remaining years of the 1870's he and Captain George Wheeler were in charge of geographic and geologic surveys that included the Waterpocket Fold area.

Powell's scientist-explorers were responsible for applying formal names to the region's major geographic features. Some of these were replaced later with names applied by local residents.

Settlement

Having settled the valleys of central Utah during the 1850's and 1860's, Mormon colonists began looking elsewhere for new worlds to support a growing population. There were open valleys to the east, but these were higher and colder. They were suitable for grazing but not ideal for farming, as settlers learned to their future distress. And they were occupied by hostile Indians.

Two groups of Mormon militia entered the area during the 1860's, even before the scientists. Their reports and that of a Mormon peace-making party in 1873 stimulated the arrival of stockraisers and settlers within a few years.

Upper valley towns to the west were settled first, during the late 1870's. Then farmers and stockmen scattered out from this nucleus to other parts of the Fremont valley, and by 1885 most of the likely town-

Early Capitol Gorge travel *NPS photo*

Doc Inglesby *Courtesy Katherine Black*

17

sites had been occupied as far east as Hanksville. Within the present boundaries of the park, Fruita and Pleasant Creek (Sleeping Rainbow-Floral Ranch) were settled within a year or two of 1880.

A harsh frontier

Life for Fremont valley pioneers resembled that of earlier Utah colonists in hardship and difficulty. Most of the area's settlers had pioneered other parts of Utah and already knew 20 or 30 years of frontier living. Whatever their background, however, few had experienced more difficulty in wresting a livelihood from the land.

The climate was severe, especially in the upper valleys near 7,000 feet. Strong winds were disagreeable. Rocks were scattered everywhere. Remoteness from population centers added loneliness to problems of supply. Roads were extremely rough for the first 40 years or so. Livestock had to be driven to distant markets, and local produce found buyers only long miles away.

The worst problem of all was a controlled water supply. Though water was comparatively plentiful here, it was not conveniently accessible. Reservoirs, canals and ditches had to be built, and these were fairly successful in the upper valleys.

In the lower valleys, where the climate is more favorable for crops, the river proved to be uncontrollable. Heartbreaking floods wiped out in hours the results of years of toil. Their fortunes lost and spirits broken, many of the lower valley's people moved away. Several of these episodes are described in the Road Logs.

In short, then, population of the Fremont valleys has always been limited to a few hundred families by climate, lack of arable land, a rugged topography, remoteness, and limited water supply. A demand for the area's minerals and widespread public knowledge of its spectacular scenery would have balanced these disadvantages sooner, but only in recent years are these assets having much economic influence.

Capitol Reef — National Monument and National Park

Though the beauty of Capitol Reef was known to everybody who saw it, it was too remote and comparatively difficult of access for widespread public knowledge. During the 1920's and 1930's local enthusiasts began promoting the "Wayne Wonderland," original descriptive name for the general area. E. P. Pectol, a prominent Torrey resident, and Joseph Hickman, a local educator, were leaders in focussing public and government attention on the Reef's scenic worth.

The result was establishment by President Franklin D. Roosevelt of Capitol Reef National Monument in 1937. At that time the monument included 37,000 acres, or that part of the Waterpocket Fold known as Capitol Reef, extending from near Torrey to Pleasant Creek.

In 1968 the monument's boundaries were greatly expanded by President Lyndon B. Johnson to include almost the entire southern length of the Waterpocket Fold. Later, in 1971, the boundaries were modified and the area was designated a national park. At present the park's area totals 242,000 acres.

18

NATURAL BACKGROUND

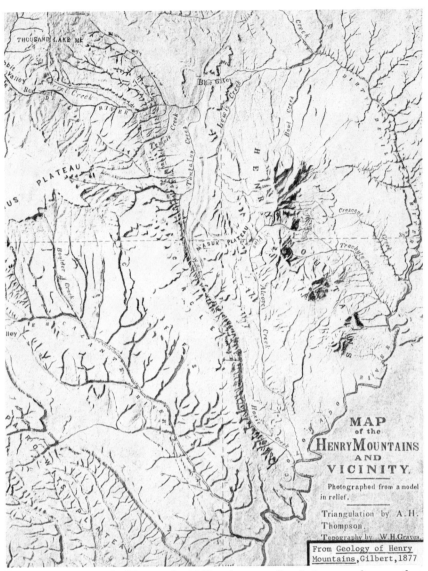

This relief model of the Waterpocket Fold and surrounding features, made more than 100 years ago by scientific explorers, has never been surpassed as a dramatic representation of the Fold country. The Waterpocket Fold, most of which is included in Capitol Reef National Park, is the central spine extending from top to bottom of the model.

A tale...a poem...a song...a divine symphony
    Capitol Reef is these, and more...
According to the viewer.

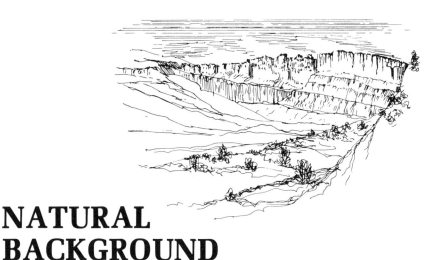

NATURAL BACKGROUND

The natural setting of Capitol Reef National Park and its immediate environs is exceptionally varied.

Much of the park consists of eroded rock that lies mostly at an elevation of 5,000 to 7,000 feet above sea level, and it receives little rain and snow. In general, vegetation is comparatively sparse except in favorable oases. Animals are present, but many of them are seldom seen by casual visitors. Certain insects may be a bother at times.

To the east and west are mountainous uplifts, rising from the park to more than 11,000 feet in altitude. These receive more moisture than the park, and they offer expanded habitat for plants and animals.

Taken together, the park and adjoining highlands represent a complex biological environment for surprisingly numerous and diversified life forms. Visitors with a liking for nature will not be disappointed here.

The Geological Story

Being so marvelously unusual, the park's rocks attract the most attention. Unusual rocks are the trademark of the entire Canyon Country; in Capitol Reef National Park and nearby, however, they are somehow "different." Why is this? There are several reasons:

1.   The park's rocks are vividly colored in an amazing range of hues. The visual and emotional impact of this unique Sleeping Rainbow differs with the viewer, of course, but most people are overwhelmed.

2.   The park's numerous rock layers, originally horizontal, have been uplifted...folded (tilted and curved)...faulted (broken and offset)...exposed to view by erosion...and then sculptured by nature into an infinitude of strange designs. The results of this sequence of crustal processes are tremendously dramatic.

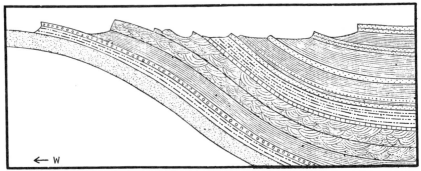

← W

Cross-section diagram of the Waterpocket Fold's rock formations in the vicinity of Mile 18, Road Log No. 4. Taken from *Geology of the Henry Mountains*, G.K. Gilbert, 1877.

3.   The rocks of the park, while marvelous in themselves, are but elements in a grand mosaic of mountains, plateaus, mesas, cliffs, canyons and numberless smaller forms. The overall combination is a matchless work of natural art.

The Waterpocket Fold

With one area of exception, the entire park consists of the exposed spine of a most remarkable geological structure known as the Waterpocket Fold. Folds in the earth's crust are not unusual; they are merely a warping, bending or flexing of rock layers. The Waterpocket Fold is such a flexure, measuring nearly 100 miles in length but only a few miles in width. It is remarkable for its great length but moreso for the manner in which its rock strata (layers or beds) have been exposed to view and then carved by erosion. Weathering has removed many thousands of feet of younger material that once buried the ancient rocks now forming the intricately sculptured backbone of the Fold.

Fremont River Canyon, traversed by Highway U-24, cuts across Capitol Reef at right angles. This provides an excellent cross-section view of the hundreds of feet of rock layers that have been "flexed" to create the great Fold. Other canyons to the south also provide such views.

The Fold extends from Thousand Lake Mountain on the north to the vicinity of Glen Canyon-Lake Powell on the south. Its central spine takes the form of a whaleback or curving slope along its eastern side; its western side is marked by lofty, near vertical cliffs. The name was given because the massive Navajo sandstone—the uppermost layer along much of the Fold—erodes in rounded contours, forming basins or "pockets" that collect and hold drainage water.

It is not known with certainty just when the Fold was created, but evidence indicates that it dates from 60 to 70 million years ago. This was shortly after the uppermost rocks still remaining to the east of the Fold were deposited in the last ocean to invade this region—in the same general period when the Rocky Mountains were created. The Henry Mountains were lifted up many millions of years later.

Capitol Reef

Capitol Reef is a section of the Waterpocket Fold (in respects its most spectacular section) extending from near Torrey to south of Pleasant Creek. In extent it coincides generally with the original Capitol Reef National Monument.

"Reef" is a term used in the west to denote a rocky ridge or barrier forming an obstruction to travel. "Capitol" is a description applied to domelike erosional forms in the Navajo sandstone along the Reef's crest. Apparently the name Capitol Reef was not in general use until the monument was created in 1937.

Reading the rocks

Rock history is a complicated subject — too much so for many visitors to the park. Nevertheless, even a superficial knowledge of the origin and position of the Fold's major rock formations (groups of similar rocks) can add immeasurably to the pleasure of a visit. It is only necessary to recognize fewer than half a dozen distinct formations in order to understand much of the Fold's basic rock structure.

As a foundation, readers should bear in mind the following:

1. Rocks are classified generally as:
Sedimentary rocks — originating as water-laid sand, pebbles, silt, mud, clay, volcanic ash, etc.; or as desert dunes. Nearly all rock formations in the park area are sedimentary in origin.
Igneous rocks — formed by volcanic action. The black volcanic boulders that are so common in the park have an igneous origin, but they came from outside the park. Igneous rock is abundant in the Henry Mountains and High Plateaus.
Metamorphic rocks — rocks that have been greatly changed from their original nature, as by heat or pressure. These are not common in the area and may be ignored here.

2. Nearly all of the park's visible sedimentary rocks were laid down over a period of 170 million years or so — between about 70 to 240 million years ago. Rocks older than that are buried. Thousands of feet of even younger rocks once covered the area but have nearly all disappeared. Exceptions are the black volcanic boulders (comparatively recent), and the loose sand and gravel of recent times (which, in turn, are the remains of older rocks). Lava caps of the High Plateaus also cover younger rocks.

3. The park's sedimentary rocks had their origin in an astonishing variety of environments, including deserts, oceans, lakes, swamps, deltas, flood plains, tidelands, and streambeds. Some formations derive from volcanic ash laid down in water. Today's rocks, the product of eons of pressure, heat and chemical action, are sandstone, mudstone, siltstone, limestone, gypsum, clay, shale, and conglomerate (a mixture of small rocks and sand).

ROCK FORMATIONS OF THE PARK AREA
From east to west along Highway U-24

Highway U-24 passes through nearly all of the park area's rock forma-
tions, from the very ancient Moenkopi between Torrey and Visitor
Center, to the Cretaceous, or youngest remaining rocks in the area, at
Caineville. The oldest of all are away from the highway, in the walls of
Sulphur Creek and Fremont River canyons.

Name of Formation	Maximum thickness (in feet)	Age (millions of years ago)	Description
Youngest rocks first: east of Capitol Reef			
Cretaceous rocks 7 different formations of sandstone, mud- stone, shale	4,000	70 to 135	Badland flats, pleated cliffs, mesas, buttes, low ridges. Muted colors: blue-gray, buff, yellow. Marine fossils.
Jurassic rocks		135 to 180	
Morrison sandstone, siltstone, conglomerate	400		Variegated Painted Desert colors; slopes, ledges and ridges. Dinosaur bones, agate
Summerville siltstone mudstone, sand- stone, gypsum	200		Numerous thin beds in cliffs and slopes. Light red-brown.
Curtis sandstone, siltstone	100		Gray-green ledges
Entrada sandstone, siltstone, claystone	800		Thin to thick beds, form- ing cliffs, monuments (Cathedral Valley); reddish brown
Carmel sandstone, claystone, siltstone, limestone, gypsum	1,000		Many beds forming cliffs, slopes, caps; yellow to gray-orange, red, green-white
Navajo sandstone	1,100		Massive cliffs, rounded domes, fins, cones (summit and east slope of Capitol Reef); white to pale-yellow
Kayenta sandstone, siltstone, conglomerate	350		Bedded, forming ter- raced ledges and low cliffs; white to red- brown

Wingate sandstone	370	Massive, forming near-vertical cliffs (west face of Capitol Reef); light-orange to red-brown
Triassic rocks	180 to 225	
Chinle siltstone, limestone, clay-stone, sandstone, conglomerate (includes Shina-rump sandstone, conglomerate)	650	Variegated colors; slopes and ledges at base of sheer Wingate cliffs. Fossils, petrified wood
Moenkopi mudstone, siltstone, sand-stone, limestone	1,000	Evenly bedded, forms low ridges, ledges, cliffs, mounds. Ripple marks. Reddish-brown, yellowish. Highway U-24 passes across these rocks west of Visitor Center
Permian rocks	225 to 240	
Kaibab limestone	350	White
Coconino sandstone	800	White to gray. These two latter formations can be seen in the walls of deep canyons west of Fruita
	11,000 ±	

25

Capitol Reef's Four Key Rock Formations near Grand Wash. *Ward Roylance photo*

FOUR KEY ROCK FORMATIONS OF CAPITOL REEF

However useful, it is not necessary for the visitor to identify all the rock characteristics in the chart entitled Rock Formations of the Park Area. A visual acquaintance with only *four* very distinctive formations will require only a few minutes of study, yet will add much more meaning to a park visit. These Four Key Formations are shown in the labeled photograph. In list form, they are:

Reading down from the top of the cliffs near the Visitor Center

1. Topmost rocks - whitish, rounded domes, fins, cones, butte-forms, cliffs. These rocks are 1,000 feet above the Visitor Center; several miles eastward, due to the slope or dip of the Waterpocket Fold, they have descended to highway level.
   Navajo sandstone
(ancient sand dunes)

   (The Navajo is separated from No. 2 by the Kayenta formation, which so resembles the rocks above and below — at least from a distance — that it is best ignored by the casual visitor.)

2. Lofty, near-vertical cliffs, orange-red, massive (non-layered), fractured and fluted.
   Wingate sandstone
(ancient sand dunes)

3. Multi-colored slopes: green, purple, brown, yellow, etc.	Chinle shale, mudstone, sandstone, siltstone (waterlaid; contains volcanic ash)
4. Chocolate-colored, many-layered "mummy cliffs," buttresses, low ridges, ledges and mounds — traversed by the highway between Visitor Center and Torrey, and by the Scenic Drive south of Visitor Center.	Moenkopi sandstone, shale, siltstone, sandstone. Ripple marks.

Plant Life

Plants are more noticeable in this park than they might be in more favorable environments. One reason for this is the striking contrast between great masses of bare rock where no plants grow, and verdant canyon bottoms where plant growth may be almost luxuriant.

Actually the park and immediate vicinity are habitat for a wide variety of interesting plant life. The unusual range in altitude, from about 5,200 feet in the park's canyons to more than 11,000 feet in the neighboring highlands, provides climatic conditions for hundreds of plant species. These range from shrubs and flowers of the lower deserts through the intermediate juniper-pinyon zone to spruce-fir-pine forests and arctic tundra of the High Plateaus. The region in general is a botanist's playground.

Most visitors note the most apparent plants. These include, of course, the large cottonwoods along the Fremont River — so breathtaking in the fall. Other streamside trees and smaller plants are the boxelder, ash, tamarisk or saltcedar, and willows. Fruita residents of earlier days planted fruit orchards, as described in the road logs.

Very apparent, too, are the countless pygmy evergreens — junipers and pinyon pines that flourish throughout the Four Corners region. These picturesque little trees cover Miner's Mountain with a seemingly solid blanket.

Among the smaller plants along the drier slopes and ledges might be mentioned ephedra or Mormon tea, buffaloberry, blackbrush, rabbitbrush, and squawbush. Wild asparagus is abundant. Yucca and prickly pear cactus are common.

Finally, after this very sketchy listing, wildflowers should not be neglected. These grow in every likely spot, on the deserts, in the valleys and canyons, and tucked away in countless niches and crannies where there might be a little sand or soil, and enough moisture.

Animal Life

Where there are plants, there is animal life. Such an arid environment may not appear, to many people, as a suitable habitat for animals; but in fact the park is home for a rather amazing variety of creatures.

Not many of them will be seen by the average visitor, for most are shy, and more than a few come out only at night.

Mule deer are the most visible of the large animals. They are so numerous that they must be controlled. Since they graze in the orchards and are not too timid here, it is not unusual for visitors to see them — particularly at dusk.

Smaller animals that may be seen occasionally include jackrabbits, cottontail rabbits, skunks, chipmunks, rock squirrels, antelope ground squirrels, marmots, field mice, kangaroo rats, pack rats, muskrats and porcupines. Beaver are found in the Fremont River and streams to the west. Rarely seen in the main area of the park, but present nearby, are cougar, bobcat, coyote, gray fox and the ringtail.

Many birds inhabit the general area, especially during warmer months. They include pinyon jays, rock wrens, sage thrashers, ravens, blackbirds, hawks, magpies, woodpeckers, horned owls, hummingbirds, bluebirds, orioles, waxwings, robins, and numerous others. Golden eagles are fairly common. Gambel's quail and chukars are in the area.

Reptiles include rattlesnakes (uncommon); harmless garter (water) snakes, which are fairly common; and bullsnakes, which are not poisonous. Lizards are common; they are harmless, of course. Horned toads, actually lizards, can be seen now and then, as can toads and frogs.

Trout frequent the river upstream from the campground.

Winter view of The Castle   *NPS photo*

Strange rock forms   *Ward Roylance photo*

Falls in Sulphur Creek Canyon *NPS photo*

South Desert   *NPS photo*

29

Climate and Seasons

Capitol Reef National Park is situated almost entirely in the Canyonlands section of the Colorado Plateau province. Canyonlands is hundreds of miles from the Pacific Ocean and Gulf of Mexico, its moisture sources; and it is almost surrounded by mountains, which capture nearly all the rain and snow that manage to get past.

Therefore Canyonlands is an arid region with low humidity. Technically it is a desert, receiving considerably less than the minimum precipitation that qualifies an area for that classification.

The Waterpocket Fold in general receives only about 7 inches of moisture per year, except for its highest points, which receive somewhat more. The Henry Mountains and the western High Plateaus capture considerably more than the park, and from the plateaus flow the park's few perennial streams. Other streambeds contain water only in spring or following a rain.

Surprisingly, the greater part of the park's annual precipitation falls during July, August and September in the form of rain. This often comes in cloudbursts that release so much water onto non-absorptive rock that it collects rapidly into countless drainage channels, pouring into the larger washes and eventually the Fremont River. Streambeds that are normally dry may then witness short-lived torrents of turbid, debris-laden floodwater. In general, floods have not been as violent during the past few decades of reduced precipitation as they were 60 or 70 years ago, but they are always impressive and can still be dangerous. This is why hikers and vehicles should avoid being caught in stream channels when a rainstorm is threatening.

Seasons

Being in the temperate zone, the park experiences four distinct seasons: spring, summer, fall and winter.

Spring and fall months are the mildest and most pleasant in temperature. In general, this is the period from late April to early June, and early September to late October. July and August are the hottest months, when the daytime temperature may reach 100 degrees F. or slightly higher. Nights are cool even in summer.

Between late October and late March the temperature may be chilly, and there is occasional snow. However, snowfall within the park usually is scanty; except in midwinter it does not normally remain long on the ground. Midwinter temperatures may fall to zero degrees F. or below.

Visitors who do not plan extensive hiking or backpacking will find that Capitol Reef is an all-year park. Main roads are open nearly all the time, rarely being snowpacked or icy. Off-highway roads may be closed temporarily after heavy rain or snow, but this usually occurs only a few days each year. Winter snow adds a very dramatic accent to the park's red rocks.

Mosquitoes, "gnats" and flies occasionally are bothersome in warmer months. Be prepared with insect repellent and light jackets.

SEEING THE PARK

Cliff and cottonwoods *NPS photo*

Cohab Canyon *NPS photo*

Goosenecks of Sulphur Creek *NPS photo*

Muley Twist Canyon *NPS photo*

SEEING THE PARK

Introduction

You can see Capitol Reef National Park from your automobile. You can see it by hiking. And you can see it from an airplane.

Those in a car will see one aspect of the park. Hikers will see another. And bird's-eye viewers will see something entirely different. All will be thrilled. The park offers something marvelous from every viewing perspective.

This book describes how to see the park from its roads and trails, with additional information about its backcountry hiking possibilities.

Some 200 miles of paved and unpaved roads within the park and immediately outside its boundaries make it possible for the sightseer to view much of the park from the comfort of a wheeled vehicle. Roads follow along the varicolored cliff-face of Capitol Reef for 20 miles, between Torrey and Pleasant Creek. Highway 24 cuts completely through the Waterpocket Fold via Fremont River Canyon, revealing its monoclinal structure in beautiful cross-section. Spur drives enter Grand Wash and Capitol Gorge. Forest roads wind across the high eastern slopes of Boulder and Thousand Lake mountains, overlooking the park from lofty vantage points. And fair-weather dirt roads parallel the eastern whaleback slope of the Fold for nearly 80 miles, giving access to its maze of tantalizing gorges and slickrock breaks.

These routes are described in detail in the descriptive road logs below. Hikers may walk any or all of the park's maintained foot trails. Measuring about 20 miles in total length, these trails are all within 10 miles of the Visitor Center. They lead into the park's magnificent canyons, climb to dizzy heights near the Reef's summit, and penetrate the weird "rock jungle."

Finally, backpackers or day hikers who don't care to hike the maintained foot trails have countless choices of where to go, how long to stay, and what type of terrain they want to tackle. Canyons of all dimensions, slickrock slopes, ridges and cliffs — hiking challenges of every description. These also are described in this section.

Whatever mode of sightseeing travel you select, be sure to refer to the checklists included in this guide to help you avoid trouble. These are:

- For all visitors: "General Park Regulations" (page 111)
- For those who drive the side roads: "Checklist for Off-Highway Vehicle Travel" (inside back cover)
- For hikers: "Safety Cautions, Regulations and Suggestions " (page 108)

South Desert   *Fran Barnes photo*

Descriptive Road Log
No. 1
SCENIC DRIVE

South From Visitor Center
Along Face of Capitol Reef

Fruita to Grand Wash, Capitol Gorge and Pleasant Creek
(Sleeping Rainbow Ranch)

The Scenic Drive is an unpaved but well maintained graveled road that extends southward along the "Sleeping Rainbow" face of Capitol Reef. Until the present highway through Fremont River gorge was completed in 1962, this was the main route of travel: by Indians from immemorial, and later, beginning in the 1870's, by white explorers, pioneers, prospectors and settlers. It is entirely suitable for passenger cars when dry, but the road may be closed to traffic when wet or snow-packed (rare).

The Drive extends 11 miles from the Visitor Center to Sleeping Rainbow (Floral) Ranch, giving access to Grand Wash, Capitol Gorge and popular hiking trails. It is a low speed drive (15 and 25 mph), ideal for leisurely sightseeing. Along the way are numerous pulloffs that invite spontaneous hiking away from the road or formal trails.

Miles from
Visitor Center

0   **Park Visitor Center** and parking area at junction of Scenic Drive and Highway U-24.

Visitor Center, an attractive structure of native sandstone, was dedicated in 1967. It offers informational services, publications, exhibits and an orientation film. Grounds feature typical native plants of the area.

The old visitor center, dating from 1938, is still in use behind the new building. Across the road to the east is the park residential area.

Giant cliffs, a thousand feet high, overlook the center on the north. The row of great white "fins" along the upper rim reminded local people of a fleet of ships entering a harbor. One of them bears the local name of "Sleeping Ute"; the resemblance is obvious. Directly north is a dramatic fluted cliff knows as The Castle.

South of the Visitor Center the road passes through an area that once contained more buildings than it does today. None of the original pioneer homes remain, but a few buildings of more recent vintage still stand.

FRUITA (elevation 5,418 feet)—For 80 years or so, between about 1880 and 1960, Fruita was a small farming hamlet of 8 or 10 families. During its first 20 years it was known as Junction, the name being changed about 1901 to Fruita.

Arable land was not sufficient to support more than a few people, but the secluded valley's climate was more moderate than that to the west and it was soon found that a variety of orchard fruits could be grown. Thus its name.

Local fruit became renowned for quality, and eventually the valley contained hundreds of trees bearing several varieties of apples, peaches and cherries, as well as Bartlett pears, apricots, and even Concord grapes. Fruit brought badly needed cash; however, distance from markets, poor roads and other problems beset the early growers. Today the orchards are maintained by the National Park Service, the fruit being harvested mainly by the public at a modest charge.

Most people took odd jobs, sold produce or livestock—anything that offered money to supplement what could be raised. They grew beans, squash, early potatoes, peas, radishes, corn, melons, etc. From sorghum cane they produced molasses. Alfalfa was grown for their animals. They raised chickens for eggs and meat. Cattle, hogs, turkeys and sheep also provided meat, as did deer, antelope, ducks and fish. During prohibition days and earlier times, a few entrepeneurs manufactured whiskey, wine and beer.

In 1937 Capitol Reef National Monument was created and Fruita became a private oasis surrounded by public land. Gradually since then the National Park Service has acquired all private land and replaced most of the old buildings with lawns, orchards, campground, picnic area, etc. Most of the former residents moved to Torrey and other nearby towns.

0.2 Park employee residence (left). Originally the house was built by and served as the part-time home for Dr. Dean R. and Lila Eccles Brimhall, prominent residents of Salt Lake City. Both were distinguished in their respective fields, Mrs. Brimhall as professor of dramatic arts at the University of Utah, Dean as a pioneer in aviation research, educator, and government administrator on federal and state levels. During the last 30 years of his life, Dean spent much of his free time at Fruita, using it as a base for exploring the wild canyon country that surrounds it, photographing and analyzing the region's prehistoric Indian rock art (rock writing).

Undoubtedly Dr. Brimhall was the first white man to view

much of this ancient art, some of which is almost inaccessible. Before his death in 1972 at the age of 85 he had become recognized as a foremost authority on that subject.

0.4 Sulphur Creek, occasionally dry, is on the left. Residents claim that early-day floods left debris as much as 20 feet above the present creek bed. Note interesting spiderweb veining of the rock ledge beside the road on right; the veins are gypsum. Capitol Dome looms ahead between canyon walls.

0.9 Buildings on left. Parking pullout to right. Formerly the "downtown" of Fruita village, this area bears little resemblance to earlier times—even to the 1930's or 1940's.

A motel occupied the opposite side of the road near the curve for about 30 years, its operator also providing guided tours. Beyond the motel, on the outside of the curve, was the home of Dr. A. L. Inglesby, who purchased land here in 1936. "Doc" Inglesby, a noted rock collector and lapidarist, became almost a legendary character during many years in Fruita and died in 1960 at an advanced age. A contemporary writer described him as "that student and disciple of Utah's back trails, explorer, philosopher, geologist and mineralogist, widely known and loved as the Sage of the Wayne Wonderland...Doc's home at Fruita is a shrine that thousands have come to know and love..."

The small cottage across the road from parking area was the studio of Richard Sprang, artist and originator of the popular comic and television characters Batman and Robin. Sprang was attracted to the area by its wild beauty. He and Elizabeth his wife, also an artist, eventually built a landmark home near Grover.

1.1 Picnic and parking area (left), on the former site of corrals and fields. Across the road, the lecture area occupies the original homesite of Neils Johnson, one of the first settlers of Fruita in the early 1880's, who drowned in the river nearby. Later the site was the home of the Chesnut family, one of whose members (Jay Chesnut) has been mayor of Torrey for a number of years.

The majestic cottonwood trees overhanging the parking area are objects of awe for most visitors. Two are among the largest and oldest specimens of their kind in Utah, at least one of them measuring 20 feet or more in circumference. Ring borings indicate the largest tree is more than 90 years old, the others a decade or two younger.

Curving around the parking-picnic area, the Fremont River cuts through Capitol Reef (Waterpocket Fold) in a canyon followed by Highway U-24. Then it passes through some of the most spectacular desert and canyon country in America before joining the Colorado River (now Lake Powell) about 40 miles below Hanksville. See Road Logs No. 2 and 3 for additional information about the river.

1.2 Parking pulloff (right) near old house and barn. A six-unit motel once stood between the barn and house. All were owned by Dewey and Nell Gifford, who lived in the house for 41 years between 1928 and 1969—the longest period of residence in Fruita, so far as known.

Part of the house dates from 1905 or thereabouts, when it was built by the Pendleton family; the barn also was built about that time. The family included some young boys, and the story is told that their father—"Old Man Pendleton"—kept them busy during winter months with fence building. The sturdy fence of lava boulders that winds along the face of the ridge behind the house is the result of this make-work project. It was used for livestock control.

Dewey and Nell Gifford raised their family here, and Dewey worked for the Park Service for 20 years. Making a living was a constant struggle. They had a large orchard and garden, and their alfalfa field and peach orchard are now occupied by the park campground. "We *had* to raise our own living," Dewey said. "We couldn't go to market and buy it. I took every cash job I could get, such as working on the roads. And I hauled and peddled fruit." Nell and two young helpers would pick as many as 80 lugs of apricots a day. Dewey would load them on his truck and sell them in distant towns. Much fruit was dried and bottled. Hams were smoked in the small building behind the house.

1.3 Cohab Canyon Trailhead (left). This moderate but very scenic trail climbs in switchbacks to a small but rugged gorge supposedly used during Fruita's earliest days as a hiding place for Mormon polygamists or "cohabitationists." See description in Trails section. In the 1880's, Mormons had not renounced the practice of plural marriage, which had then become a federal offense. Several polygamist families lived in Fruita for a time, others in nearby towns, and apparently polygamists from other parts of Utah found refuge from federal marshals in rugged Wayne County during the years of prosecution. Many of them, unwilling to give up their families and religious beliefs, eventually moved into Mexico through this area.

1.4 *Main campground.* In an attractive setting of orchards, fields and lawns, the campground features 53 camping units (tables, charcoal firestands). Two restrooms with running water. Drinking water. No trailer hookups. Ground fires not allowed. The campground is a fee area, and in summer months is nearly always filled by early afternoon. Sites are assigned on a first-come, first-served basis. Open all year.

To the south of the campground entrance is a low mound, against the south side of which are the remains of an *old lime kiln.* The kiln was used for converting limestone—obtained from canyons to the west—into slaked lime, an ingredient of plaster and mortar.

Campground near Visitor Center   *Fran Barnes photo*

Continuing south, the road passes an apricot orchard and an open area once occupied by fields, orchards and several buildings. Ahead the road ascends Danish Hill, so named — according to Charles Kelly — because "Two Danishmen were traveling through with a team of poor horses and a broken down outfit... (on this incline) a bolt through the doubletrees broke and their wagon slid back down the grade, wrecking it."

1.6   End of pavement. Beyond this point the road is graded and graveled. It may be closed to travel when exceptionally wet.

2.6   Parking area (R) at crest of Danish Hill. This is a choice spot for viewing Fruita valley and the face of Capitol Reef to north and south. Short hikes to either side of the road provide even better views. Fern's Nipple is   prominent on top of the Reef ahead. Note curious standing rocks known as demoiselles scattered along rocky slopes at the cliff's base. The vividly colored Chinle formation is distinctive in this vicinity.

Beyond this crest the road descends toward Grand Wash, a great gash in the cliffs ahead.

3.5   Junction with road leading left into Grand Wash, also known as Grand Gorge, one of the most scenically dramatic canyons along the Reef. *Do not enter in wet or threatening weather!* The streambed is normally dry, but the canyon itself is evidence that

39

this has not always been the case. Along the Grand Wash road:
Miles

0.2 On the left-hand cliff (north), near the mouth of the wash, are tunnels marking the Oyler uranium mine. *Danger: keep out!* Tom Nixon, "Tine" Oyler, and others took a small quantity of uranium ore from these tunnels at various times. A little uranium ore also was mined from claims known as the Yellowbird, on the opposite side of the canyon. Numerous prospect holes were cut into the Reef at other spots during the frantic uranium rush of the 1950's. At that time a national monument, Capitol Reef was opened to uranium prospecting and mining, the only national park area to be so violated. No commercial deposits were located.

1.0 Shinob Canyon (R), a ruggedly picturesque gorge in the south wall of Grand Wash, makes an interesting hike. In the other direction a sign points toward Cassidy Arch, high in the north wall of the main canyon, toward the west.

1.2 End of road and parking area. In the south wall is a huge, shallow cavity known as Echo Cliff, also as Singing Rock, where dedication ceremonies were held in 1937 when the monument was created.

Trail leads along the wash to The Narrows (1.3 mile) and eventually (2¼ miles) to Highway U-24. See page 89 for description. This trail also gives access to Cassidy Arch and Frying Pan trail (see page 93).

Return to junction.

3.5 Continue south from Grand Wash on main road. Note that the Wingate sandstone, which forms the high vertical cliff, does not have the same red-brown or orange color that predominates farther to the northwest. Here its color is a subtler shade, with attractive banding or striped effects. Columnar fluting, caused by vertical fracturing, is splendid along the cliff face south of here.

6.1 Parking area (R) at a summit known as Slickrock Divide. This is a choice panoramic viewpoint. Not only does the Reef appear in grand perspective, but the great rounded profile of Miner's Mountain is very impressive here. Named for its mineral deposits (copper and uranium, primarily), the uplift is a part of the Waterpocket Fold. Its rocks are older than those in the face of the Reef, which once extended up and over the dark wooded slopes you now see.

Note the covering of pygmy evergreens (pinyon pine and juniper), the characteristic trees of this region. Also take note of the area's interesting "ripple rock," slabs of layered Moenkopi sandstone. The ripple marks are evidence that this rock originated as sand at the margin of an ancient body of water.

Short hikes to the left, along the cliff, or to the right up Miner's Mountain, are very rewarding. To the south, the dark brown Moenkopi ridge becomes higher; it is capped by light colored Shinarump sandstone, which has broken off along the edge and tumbled as blocks and boulders onto the slopes below. These Shinarump fragments have weathered into fantastic shapes and patterns.

7.0 Parking turnoff (R). Weirdly eroded Shinarump boulders line the roadside. One in particular, closest to the road on the left, resembles an armored dinosaur. The famed Egyptian Temple, a beautifully designed Moenkopi cliff, looms above the road on the left. Its striking resemblance to Egyptian architecture is more apparent at the next pulloff. A short hike up the low ridge on right affords an especially fine view.

7.3 Parking turnoff (L). Egyptian Temple, formerly known as Organ Rock, appears in its most stately aspect to the north. It is carved in the same Moenkopi rock formation that is so impressive in the Fluted (Mummy) Cliffs along Highway U-24 between the Visitor Center and Bicknell. The Shinarump sandstone cap on top of the Temple here vividly illustrates the slope or tilt of the Waterpocket Fold.

The low ridge to the right (west) is an ideal site for photographing the Temple and cliffs. A short hike into the huge amphitheater on the eastern cliff rewards the explorer with voice echoes and strange erosional forms.

Ahead, the road descends toward the yawning mouth of Capitol Gorge.

8.3 Junction: Capitol Gorge straight ahead; Sleeping Rainbow (Floral) Ranch, right. The great fluted crest to the right is Eph Hanks Tower, named for the noted pioneer scout who settled Floral Ranch (see below).

The Exhibit Shelter features interpretive displays that describe the geology, water erosion, plants, wildlife and human history of Capitol Gorge. Toilets nearby.

Do not enter Capitol Gorge in wet or threatening weather! Road may be closed when wet or dangerous.

The road into the Capitol Gorge is the original highway through Capitol Reef, first opened to vehicle travel in the mid-1880's by E. C. Behunin, Walter Hanks and other local men. Until 1962 it served as a state road, causing more maintenance problems, perhaps, than any other important highway in the state because every major storm would wash it out in places or cover it with boulders. Despite these handicaps, it offered the shortest, most feasible pass through the Reef for 80 years.

The road ends at a parking area 2 miles from the junction. Along the way it passes through an ever-narrowing, winding, profoundly deep gorge, between sheer sandstone walls. These massive surfaces have been carved by water into exquisite three-dimensional art reliefs—natural designs of marvelous intricacy, elegance and symmetry. Seeping water has added tonal coloring to the cliffs as desert varnish "tapestry."

A sign marks the vicinity where with a very short walk it is possible to see the majestic Golden Throne, high above through a notch in the north wall.

Details of the Capitol Gorge and Golden Throne hiking trails, and other attractions in the canyon, can be found in the Trails chapter.

8.3   Return to junction. The road continues south to Sleeping Rainbow (Floral) Ranch on Pleasant Creek. In good weather, high-clearance vehicles (preferably 4-wheel-drive) can be driven beyond the ranch to Tantalus Flats, Lower Bown's Reservoir, and the Torrey-Boulder road. This route gives hiking access to the east end of Sheets Gulch and Oak Creek Canyon, routes that might appeal to rugged hikers, described more fully in the Hiking chapter. Inquire from rangers or at Visitor Center before attempting.

About 1 mile south of the Capitol Gorge junction is Golden Throne View parking area (L), which affords a spectacular view of this noble butte-form and companions of comparable majesty.

11.4 **Sleeping Rainbow Ranch.** Until 1978, when it became part of the park, Sleeping Rainbow Ranch was private property. Part of the ranch, on a ridge overlooking Pleasant Creek valley, continues to be occupied by its most recent owners, Lurt and Alice Knee. Admission to that area is restricted. However, park visitors may visit the remainder of the ranch in the valley along the stream, where the original pioneer fields, orchards and homes were located. Little remains to indicate its early appearance.

Lurt and Alice Knee are known by thousands of visitors to this area, having operated a tour service and guest ranch for decades. The Knees have lived in this beautiful valley longer than anybody else.

Lurt purchased the ranch in 1939, bestowing the name of Sleeping Rainbow, and Alice joined him some years later.

Together they built their guest and tour service into a flourishing operation, and through it introduced nature photographers and travel writers not only to Capitol Reef and the Waterpocket Fold, but to the little known country surrounding them.

By hosting the right people for 40 years and pioneering sightseeing travel to formerly remote and little known points of interest, the Knees were instrumental in publicizing and opening up a large part of western Canyonlands to travel by the general public.

Floral Ranch, the pioneer name for this valley, was settled in 1882 by Ephraim K. and Thisbe Hanks and their large family. Several other families joined them at that time or later. Eph Hanks had already become somewhat of a legend among his fellow Mormons when he brought his family to this place, which Mrs. Hanks named Floral Ranch for its wild flowers.

The following story of "Eph" Hanks is related at length to illustrate the type of people who settled this frontier a hundred years ago. Thisbe his wife bore 12 children. Their friends and neighbors, E. C. and Jane Behunin (mentioned elsewhere) had a family of 13 children, born in 9 different places. Eph's cousin Ebenezer Hanks was the first settler of Hanksville in 1883 and died there the following year. All of them—men, women and children—were true pioneers on a harsh frontier, in a land that Lurt Knee terms "awesome and unforgiving."

In his teens Eph was a sailor. After joining the Mormon Church in its youthful years he marched with the Mormon Battalion during the Mexican War on its epic journey from the Missouri River to southern California. He carried mail across the plains from Utah to Missouri during the 1850's, and helped to save a freezing and starving party of handcart emigrants in 1856.

During the so-called Utah War in 1857-58 he was a Mormon scout, harassing federal troops and serving as a spy. According to one account, "So daring was he... that the bravest men in his company were not anxious to follow him... One dark night he crawled so near to the army officers' tents that the cook unwittingly threw scraps from the general's table over him."

He served as a Mormon missionary to the Indians. He engaged in trading, lumbering, manufacturing and mining. He was a blacksmith and farmer, and he built perhaps a dozen houses for his families in at least six different places. It is said that he was the first man to discover silver-quartz ore on the site of the immensely productive Silver King mine at Park City; but he never was financially successful at mining.

In his personal life, Eph Hanks was just as unusual. He married four wives as a Mormon polygamist and fathered 26 children by three of them; however, three of his wives divorced him many years before he settled at Pleasant Creek. Despite local tradition, only one family accompanied him there.

Always a faithful Mormon, Ephraim Hanks became a Patriarch in his later years. He was a renowned healer, revered as having performed many miracles. His son Walter served 18 years as the one and only Mormon bishop of Caineville, never being late for a meeting.

A friend, Dave Rust, said Eph Hanks once delivered the most memorable prayer he had ever heard—the "prayer of my life"—as follows: "O Lord, we have come here to learn something. Bless us to that end, Amen."

In 1877 Brigham Young asked Eph and Thisbe to take charge of the Mormon ferry operation at Lee's Ferry, Arizona. They settled instead at Burrville, about 40 miles west of Capitol Reef, Brigham Young having died in the meantime. This location was too cold, however, and many of their cattle died there in the winter of 1881-82. The following spring Eph and two of his sons visited Pleasant Creek.

Reporting to Thisbe on what they discovered, one son wrote later, Eph told her that "He'd found the most beautiful country that God ever made...in a fierce, primitive way that stole your breath and made your head light." But when Thisbe saw it "she cried tears of disappointment and discouragement." That first winter the family of 10 lived in a temporary log shelter built against the cliff.

Before Eph died in 1896, he and his family built better homes of logs and boards. They planted gardens and hundreds of fruit trees. But though the valley was beautiful it was too small to support many people, and eventually all of the family moved away. Their places were taken by others until finally Lurt Knee came in 1939.

Eph Hanks Tower *Fran Barnes photo*

Descriptive Road Log
No. 2

WEST ON UTAH HIGHWAY 24
From Park Visitor Center
(To Torrey - Bicknell - Loa)

Utah Highway 24 is a good, moderate-speed, all-weather paved road. Between the Visitor Center at Fruita and Torrey, a distance of 11 miles, it climbs about 1400 feet. The highway parallels the base of brightly colored Capitol Reef for much of the distance. Near Torrey the cliff face blossoms into truly magnificent "breaks" of varicolored, beautifully sculptured buttes, ledges and tiers of stepped cliffs that soar upwards toward the summit of Thousand Lake Mountain.

Miles from
Visitor Center *

0 (81)   Park Visitor Center and parking area at junction of U-24 and Scenic Drive leading to Fruita, Grand Wash, Capitol Gorge and Sleeping Rainbow Ranch (see Road Log No. 1).

.2 (80.8)   Bridge across Sulphur Creek, a tributary of the Fremont River. Ordinarily a small stream, or completely dry, the creek may become a torrent during summer rainstorms. Originally known as Sand Creek by local people, Sulphur Creek joins the Fremont about a mile downstream.

1.0 (80)   Milepost and parking turnoff (left). Note especially The Castle, a detached butte of fluted Wingate sandstone often pictured in publications. The greenish-black ridge beyond the Visitor Center, covered with dark boulders, is Johnson Mesa, also known as Black Ridge. It separates Sulphur Creek from the Fremont River. Note the luxuriant vegetation along the valley floor, where water is available to help it flourish.

*Mileages in parentheses — example: (80.8) — are milepost readings. Tenths-of-a-mile in these readings are approximate. Mileposts or mileage markers are located along the south side of the highway. Take note of your car's odometer reading at beginning of tour.

Note also the exceptional thickness of the greenish Chinle and red-brown Moenkopi rocks in this vicinity. The Shinarump sandstone, which appears several miles farther west, is missing here.

This is a convenient location for becoming familiar with, or reviewing, the four basic rock formations that give the face of Capitol Reef its special personality. The short time necessary to learn the names and relationships of these rock groups will more than repay itself in increased enjoyment and understanding. See page 26.

The road ascends rather steeply from Sulphur Creek, climbing 700 feet in 2 miles.

1.8 (79.2) Parking turnoff (left). The steepest cimb in this vicinity, on the old road near the present highway, was known by local people as Ford Hill, so named because early Model T Fords sometimes found it necessary to back up the hill in reverse gear so that gasoline would reach the carburetor.

The magnificent face of Capitol Reef can be seen here in a comprehensive panoramic sweep.

Several rock formations are unusually massive in this area, particularly the sheer orange Wingate cliffs, surmounting a grand exposure of greenish Chinle and layered, red-brown Moenkopi. Together, they rise more than 1,000 feet above the road.

Here the Moenkopi forms a buttressed cliff known as the Fluted Wall or Mummy Cliff. On the promontory ridge ahead, some Moenkopi "mummies" have collapsed, leaving a sheer wall in places. The Chimney Rock Trail winds along the upper edge of this ridge.

The tilt or monoclinal slope of the Waterpocket Fold system is quite apparent for several miles in this vicinity.

At the base of the cliffs to the east is an expanse of fairly level ground known as Whiskey Flat, so called because it was the site of a memorable alcoholic "binge" by a party of travelers during Prohibition days.

2.4 (78.6) Summit of 2-mile grade from Visitor Center. It is suggested that eastbound travelers shift into a lower gear here for at least part of the 700-foot descent.

2.7 (78.3) Junction with sideroad leading to Panorama Point and Goosenecks Point.

Panorama Point parking area, 0.1 mile, then a short walk to overlook point. Full-circle panoramic sweep of Capitol Reef's face, the Henry Mountains beyond, Chimney Rock, Torrey Knoll and Thousand Lake Mountain to the west, and the grand swell of Miner's Mountain—in short, just about everything described in this log. The Point affords one of the park's most comprehensive overlooks.

Goosenecks Point, 1.0 mile to parking area, affords a

dizzy look down into the winding gorge of Sulphur Creek, about 500 precipitous feet below. See page 88 in Hiking chapter for description.

3   (78)   Milepost and parking turnoff. Good view of Chimney Rock in profile. Chimney Rock spire, detached by erosion from the main cliff, consists of a layered Moenkopi base capped by a precariously balanced block of more resistant Shinarump sandstone. The Shinarump gives some protection to the underlying rock. Chimney Rock rises about 200 feet above its base.

Chimney Rock Trail winds along the crest of the high bluff above the butte. Note that the red-brown, many-layered Moenkopi formation is the basement rock all along the highway between Fruita and Torrey. Deep canyons of Sulphur Creek to the south, visible in this vicinity, are carved in Moenkopi in their upper levels.

3.2   (77.8)   Parking area for Chimney Rock Trail (right).

The route is a fairly strenuous 3.4-mile hike requiring several hours. See page 90 for description of this route and Spring Canyon extension.

4   (77)   Milepost and parking turnoff. Interpretive marker. Standing out from a small Moenkopi ridge to the south is a curious erosional form known locally as Old Man Pendleton or the Silent Watchman, more formally as The Motorman.

An interpretive marker describes an interesting geological fault (a crustal break where opposing rocks have been offset by uplifting and/or downdropping). The fault can be seen where the Chimney Rock Trail climbs the green Chinle in a gap to the left of Chimney Rock: rocks on the right of the gap are 165 feet higher than corresponding rocks on the left.

Note deep gorges of Sulphur Creek to the south, and the grand amphitheater of Chimney Rock to the north.

5.2   (75.8)   Parking turnoff. Across the highway loom two great chunks of buff-colored Shinarump sandstone known as Twin Rocks.

The Shinarump, which forms a ledge here, caps Chimney Rock to the east but gradually pinches out (disappears) closer to the Visitor Center. A member of the Chinle formation, the Shinarump is quite prominent from here westward.

Note changing characteristics of the orange Wingate cliffs that tower overhead. In places they are highly fractured and fluted, in other places not so much. To the east they are capped by domes of Navajo sandstone; here the Navajo has receded beyond sight to the north. Note enormous arch-forms in the cliff face. They might be termed "arches in embryo."

The old Fruita-Torrey road, now abandoned, can be seen to the south.

In both directions from Twin Rocks, close to the highway, are deformed rocks caused by faulting. Normally the layers of basement rock along the road here (Moenkopi) are tilted upwards toward the south, downwards toward the cliff. In this vicinity, however, the tilt reverses directions. In several places the Moenkopi layers form a "V"; in another spot, beside the highway, the rock has been metamorphosed — changed by heat and pressure.

6.3   (74.7)   West entrance to Capitol Reef National Park (sign). Parking turnoff (left).

To the east is a fine panorama of Capitol Reef, its rainbow cliffs and dramatic summit domes and cones. Behind the Reef loom several peaks of the remote Henry Mountains, a regional landmark and one of the famed "Island Ranges" of Canyonlands. See Road Log No. 4 for description.

Note the uncommonly expansive and colorful exposures of greenish-gray Chinle rocks along the cliff base in this area.

Adding a pleasant accent to the landscape are pygmy evergreens — junipers and pinyon pines. Normally occurring together, they are the most common trees of the Colorado Plateau. Other plants seen along the highway include rabbitbrush, which puts on a golden display in fall; ephedra or Mormon (Brigham) tea; black brush; and a variety of flowers.

6.9   (74.1)   Large parking area, sometimes used for overnight camping (left).

Here the highway moves away from the cliff into the broad upper valley of the Fremont River, which lies at an altitude of more than 6,500 feet. The lofty bulk of Boulder Mountain (Aquarius Plateau) looms against the southern sky, that of Thousand Lake Mountain to the north.

A short distance west, U-24 crosses the wash of Sulphur Creek, a normally dry stream which rises on Thousand Lake Mountain and joins the Fremont River at Fruita. Sulphur Creek enters the valley here in a deep gorge. In this area, rainbow colors and erosional drama of the Waterpocket Fold system attain a visual and geological climax known as Torrey Breaks.

TORREY BREAKS

Rocks here have been lifted at least a thousand feet higher than they are at Fruita, by the crustal uplift that created Thousand Lake Mountain, and erosion has exposed them all in an unbelievable concentration of fluted walls and buttressed cathedrals, red buttes, multicolored Chinle slopes, orange Wingate cliffs, white Navajo domes, and even younger rocks peeping out from the mountain's dark volcanic mass. Accenting the brilliant rock colors, green pygmy evergreens sprout from every likely crevice at lower levels. White-boled aspen, ponderosa pine and other plants clothe the mountain's higher reaches.

Surely this grand combination of so many different rock types, in so many colors and erosional designs, and in such tremendous thickness ranks Torrey Breaks among Utah's superlative natural treasures.

Torrey Butte is the high red promontory on the left, rising 1,500 feet above its base.

7.1 (73.9) Rough road leading northwest (right) into Sulphur Creek gorge and Fishlake National Forest. A "w"-shaped notch in the rim of the highest cliffs to the right gives hiking access to the upper reaches of Spring Canyon   (see page 101 for hiking description).

8.0 (73) Rim Rock Motel, situated on a scenic ridge overlooking Torrey Breaks and the valley of Sand Creek. Motel, restaurant, trailer park. Vehicle tours of the park and surrounding area, in 4-wheel-drive station wagons. Address: Torrey, Utah 84775. Telephone: (801) 425-3843.

Torrey Breaks   *Ward Roylance photo*

8.5 (72.5) Parking turnoff and scenic viewpoint (left). Unpaved road winding off toward the east is the original road between Torrey and Fruita.

9.5 (71.5) Unpaved road leading eastward through former dump area into rugged Beas Lewis Flats (left). Named for Beason Lewis, an early Mormon stockman, the Flats are a high peninsula between Fremont River and Sulphur Creek. Rough dirt roads give access to a maze of ever-deepening draws, gullies and canyons, mostly cut into the red-brown Moenkopi formation.

10 (71) Junction with paved road (left) leading to Grover, Boulder, Escalante and Bryce Canyon National Park. See description at end of this log, below.

Torrey cemetery is beside this junction. To the west is a lovely panorama of green alfalfa fields, meadows, and groves of trees that mark Torrey, the community nearest to park headquarters.

11 (70) **TORREY** (eleva. 6,840 feet, about 100 population).

Milepost is located on south side of highway, midway between the Mormon chapel and Chuckwagon Store-Motel.

Torrey is a motley mix of rural rusticity and modernity — a curious blend of the old and new, ugly and attractive. The picturesque townsite, on a high bench, is marked by a luxuriant growth of huge cottonwood, poplar and evergreen trees, which thrive on water from an open canal. Many of these trees are very old, having been planted during the town's youth, 70 or 80 years ago. They are responsible in large degree for Torrey's distinctive charm.

The Torrey area was first settled by Mormon farmers and stockraisers in the 1880's. Known variously in early days as Poverty Flat and Central, Bonita and Youngstown, it received the name Torrey in 1898 when a post office was opened.

The town flourished for several decades but joined myriad other rural communities in a decline beginning about 50 years ago. In recent years there is a revival of sorts.

Three Mormon chapels in the center of town form an unusual building complex representing distinct eras and architectural styles. The log structure dates from about 1900, the large rock building from 1928, and the modern chapel from 1974. One block north is a two-story rock building dating from 1917; this was the local schoolhouse for many years.

Services-Chuckwagon Motel-General Store-Trailer Park. Tom's Service (gasoline, auto service, trailer park); Bridle Bit Cafe-Bar (also gasoline). Address: Torrey, Utah 84775.

11.7 (69.3) Access road to Fishlake National Forest and Thousand Lake Mountain (right). This very rough and steep dirt road (closed in winter) gives access to the heights of Thousand Lake Mountain. *Not recommended for ordinary passenger cars*, though 4-wheel-drive is not required when road is dry.

The right fork through Holt Draw climbs the mountain's east slope to about 8,500 feet, overlooking the fantastically rugged crest of Capitol Reef and northern Waterpocket Fold in a magnificent panorama. Also visible is the Caineville mesa and reef country, as well as Cathedral Valley and parts of the San Rafael Swell. This road ends at Paradise Flats, about 13 miles from Torrey. Backcountry hikers find this road gives convenient access to the upper breaks of Waterpocket Fold.

Lower on the mountain, other roads branch off to the west. One winds along the Velvet Ridge above Fremont River, eventually descending into Rabbit Valley near Bicknell. Another fork climbs up Sand Creek canyon to Hells Hole. From these routes, short side roads lead to the base of Chinle-Wingate cliffs where petrified wood can still be found in fragments.

Obtain detailed information about these roads from Fishlake National Forest offices in Loa and Richfield.

Twisted Juniper root   *Fran Barnes photo*

51

WEST OF TORREY

State 24 west of Torrey traverses the valley of Fremont River to **Bicknell** (8 miles), **Lyman** (13 miles), and **Loa,** the Wayne County seat (16 miles). A few miles from Loa is **Fremont,** gateway to the upper Fremont River country, Thousand Lake Mountain and Cathedral Valley (see Road Log No. 5).

These upper-valley towns were settled a few years earlier than places to the east, during the 1870's. They are clean, attractive communities, having obvious civic pride.

About 3½ miles west of Torrey, a paved side road leads to **Teasdale,** a quiet, pleasant village nestled against Boulder Mountain. This short spur offers one of the area's superb visual experiences — a full-face view of Thousand Lake Mountain and its soaring foundation of brilliantly colored, terraced cliffs, climbing toward the mountain's flat crest nearly 5,000 feet above. On either side are sentinel buttes, black and white Ant Hill dome on the west (9,300 feet), Torrey Knoll on the east (8,200 feet).

THE RED GATE AND FREMONT RIVER

The town of **Bicknell** marks a dramatic zone of transition between dark, lava-colored slopes and valleys of the High Plateaus and brilliantly colored sedimentary forms of the Canyonlands region. Thousand Lake Fault has broken the earth's crust here, downdropping on the west and burying the painted sedimentary rocks, raising them on the east and creating a strata-offset of several thousand feet.

Three miles east of Bicknell the Fremont River cuts a gateway between Thousand Lake Mountain and Aquarius Plateau (Boulder Mountain). This vividly colored pass was named the Red Gate by geographer-explorers of the 1870's, and the lovely sculptured cliffs beyond were called The Fluted Wall — names that still apply today.

The Fremont River has its source in Fish Lake and nearby waters, at more than 9,000 feet above sea level. In its upper reaches the Fremont is a clear stream, habitat for trout. After it reaches younger, softer rocks east of Capitol Reef, however, it muddies rapidly.

At Hanksville the Fremont merges with Muddy Creek. The combined stream below there is known as the Dirty Devil, so named by Major Powell's river expedition in 1869. (The Fremont itself was named after explorer John Charles Fremont, who passed through its headwaters area in the early 1850's.)

Though the Fremont-Dirty Devil is only a modest stream — hardly more than a creek by eastern standards — it is one of the world's remarkable streams in terms of erosional accomplishment and the incredible terrain through which it flows. Dropping from more than 9,000 feet at its forested source to 3,600 feet at its mouth, in a distance of only 150 miles or so, the Fremont cuts a channel through lofty volcanic plateaus, verdant mountain valleys, red-rock uplifts, sandstone gorges and painted deserts.

Services in Upper Valley (west of Torrey):
Teasdale-Store, gasoline. District Ranger, Dixie National Forest.
Bicknell-Stores, cafes, motels, service stations, garage.
Lyman-Store, gasoline.
Loa-Stores, restaurant, motels, service stations, garages.
　　District Ranger, Fishlake National Forest.
Fremont-Store, gasoline.

GLACIERS AND BOULDERS

The black boulders scattered across the landscape, in the upper valleys and eastward through the park, are erosional remnants of the lava that caps Boulder and Thousand Lake mountains. Black is their natural color; white is a mineral (lime) coating deposited on that part of a boulder that might be buried in the ground. The boulders have been moved by glaciers, streams and gravity. Many boulders, no doubt, have merely been "set down" by eroding away of softer rocks that once supported them.

Small glaciers capped the nearby plateaus at times during the past few hundred thousand years — most recently only 10,000 years or so. Geologists can read the signs they left, including the area's many alpine lakes and ponds, gravel deposits, boulder drifts, and basin scouring. Local streams undoubtedly were much larger than they are today. Boulders and other erosional debris were scattered far and wide, and stream channels were deepened considerably.

BOULDER MOUNTAIN (AQUARIUS PLATEAU) ROAD
Torrey to Boulder
(Obtain maps and information from District Ranger,
Dixie National Forest, Teasdale, Utah 84773)

Long a favorite of the more adventuresome travelers, this mostly unpaved alpine drive offers some of America's sublimest red-rock views. The 40-mile road is gradually being improved; though about 20 miles have been paved or widened and graded, the remaining 20 miles are still rough and narrow but passable to ordinary cars from spring to late fall. *Caution: Watch for logging trucks along this road, especially on blind curves!*

The road branches south from U-24 one mile east of Torrey and is paved to the boundary of Dixie National Forest near picturesque Grover. From there, at 7,100 feet, it climbs the east shoulder of Boulder Mountain to altitudes of more than 9,000 feet. Trees obscure the view to a frustrating extent, but from partial clearings there are tantalizing views of a chaotic landscape so unique in form and color that belief is temporarily suspended.

Capitol Reef's domes are visible, and the pastel Caineville mesas. Across the middle ground, Waterpocket Fold stretches from north to south, its sawtooth ridge broken by deep gorges and grand buttes. The Fold's western cliff-face is dramatically apparent here, expanding into brilliant promontories and ridges of Tantalus Flats, then bending southward into the canyoned breaks of the Circle Cliffs. Looming against the eastern sky are the ever-dominant Henrys. Lower Bown's Reservoir, a popular fishing lake on a slope below the road, adds a striking contrast of blue.

As the road continues south, the Circle Cliffs come into fuller view, and then the wonderful white breaks of the upper Escalante-Boulder Creek country. Navajo Mountain can be seen nearly 100 hazy miles away beyond the Straight Cliffs of Kaiparowits Plateau.

Dixie National Forest maintains three excellent campgrounds along the road, at Singletree, Pleasant Creek and Oak Creek. All have tables, toilets and water. The summit of the Aquarius Plateau, Boulder Top, can be reached by trail from several spots. There, at 11,000 feet, is one of the highest spruce forests in the world, and a true plateau surface of glacial lakes and alpine tundra.

BOULDER (elev. 6,000 feet) has a dream-location on the south slope of the Aquarius, surrounded by stately mounds and ridges of white Navajo sandstone. A ranching and farming hamlet, it dates from later decades of the last century. Until the 1930's, when auto roads were built to connect it with the outside world, Boulder was accessible only by rough wagon road and trails. Today it can be reached by paved highway from Escalante and the unpaved mountain road from Torrey. **Services:** gasoline, groceries, motels.

East from Boulder, a good graded road through the Circle Cliffs gives access to Burr Trail, the South District of Capitol Reef National Park, the Henry Mountains, and Lake Powell (Bullfrog Marina-Resort). See Road Log No. 4 for description.

In Boulder is **Anasazi Indian Village State Historical Monument,** an attractive visitor center-museum at the site of an ancient Indian village. The museum features interpretive displays, publications, and a reconstructed Anasazi dwelling.

Known originally as the Coombs Site, the Village was occupied about 800 or 900 years ago by as many as 200 Indians of the Anasazi culture. This Pueblo culture reached its height at Mesa Verde and other places on the east side of the Colorado River, and the Coombs Site was one of the northernmost and westernmost outposts of that advanced culture. (The contemporary Fremont culture — which differed in respects from the Anasazi — flourished only a short distance away, in the Fremont River valley to the north.)

The Boulder Anasazi abandoned their settlement about 1200 A.D.; it was burned about the same time. The ruins were excavated by the University of Utah in 1958-59, and the visitor center was completed in 1970 as part of the Utah State Park system.

CAPITOL REEF - a poem waiting for a thousand poets

Descriptive Road Log
No. 3

EAST ON UTAH HIGHWAY 24
From Park Visitor Center
(Toward Notom turnoff, Caineville and Hanksville)

Utah Highway 24 is a good, all-weather paved road that follows the deep canyon of Fremont River through the park. The road provides travelers with an excellent "cross-section view" of the Waterpocket Fold's tilted rock formations. Eastward beyond the park's boundaries the road enters a region of Painted Desert badlands — an open country affording vistas of multicolored cliffs, mesas, buttes, the Henry Mountains, and the sculptured east slope of the Waterpocket Fold.

Miles from
Visitor Center

0 (81) Park Visitor Center and parking area at junction of U-24 and Scenic Drive leading to Fruita, Grand Wash, Capitol Gorge and Sleeping Rainbow (Floral) Ranch (See Road Log No. 1.)

From the Visitor Center the highway enters Fremont River Canyon, between a majestic cliff looming on the left, Sulphur Creek on the right.

0.8 (81.6) Historic Fruita Schoolhouse, a quaint wood structure built in 1896, which served for many years as the community's one-room schoolhouse, meetinghouse and social center.

Fruit orchards flourish along the canyon floor for the next mile. Dating from early days, these orchards provided food and money crops for residents. Today they are maintained by the Park Service as a part of the historic scene. See Road Log No. 1 for details.

Sulphur Creek meets Fremont River a short distance to the east. Rim Overlook Point is almost a thousand feet directly above the schoolhouse building; it is reached by foot trail from the Hickman Bridge parking area, 1 mile ahead.

1.0 (81.9) Frame house against cliff to left, almost hidden by trees, was built in the early days of Fruita. Later it was remodeled and served as the home for many years of Charles Kelly, first superintendent of Capitol Reef National Monument. A noted student of western Americana, Mr. Kelly authored numerous books and articles on western history and Utah.

1.1 (82) Parking turnoff and short trail (left). On the cliff face above a rock slope is a mural of prehistoric Fremont Indian rock art or rock writing.

When incised into the rock, such figures are known as petroglyphs (rock writing); when painted on the surface they are known as pictographs. In the park they are often a combination of both techniques and probably date from at least 800 years ago.

The park contains a number of sites where Indians of the ancient Fremont culture left a record of their presence on the rocks. Some have been badly vandalized. Visitors are asked to respect their historic value and fragility by not mutilating them in any way.

1.4 (82.3) Parking turnoff (right). Capitol Dome looms ahead, seemingly blocking the canyon from wall to wall. This impressive butte-form of Navajo sandstone actually is a "fin" when viewed from the end; it is a dome only in profile. Such visual phenomena are typical of Capitol Reef, where appearances can change dramatically with changes in perspective.

1.9 (82.8) Large parking turnoff (left). Trailhead for Hickman Bridge, Whiskey Spring and Rim Overlook trails. Across the highway is the eastern terminus of Cohab Canyon Trail. See Trails section for description.

The highway crosses Fremont River here; henceforth the river is on the left (north) for many miles.

2.1 (83) Parking turnoff (left) in curve of canyon. Fine views from here of spectacular Navajo erosional forms. These massive natural sculptures in light-colored sandstone have descended close to the road in this vicinity; only 2 miles away, above the Visitor Center, they are hundreds of feet higher, atop the Wingate and Chinle cliffs. Here the Wingate and Chinle have disappeared beneath the ground, due to the downward slope of the Waterpocket Fold.

Navajo forms to the north, above the Hickman Bridge Trail, are truly magnificent in scale and design. The swirled cone is known as Navajo Dome; together with the great Gothic arch to its left, it resembles the dome and entrance of an idealized house of worship.

(Park personnel encourage visitors to create their own similes and apply their own name choices to the park's features, most of which bear no formal names.)

The Navajo sandstone is common throughout southern Utah and northern Arizona, forming the cliff-walls of Glen Canyon and the lower Escalante system; the upper Escalante canyons near Boulder; and the tremendous cliffs and canyons of Zion National Park, where it is several thousand feet thick. The Navajo forms in this vicinity somewhat resemble those of Zion's eastern (Carmel) section.

2.5 (83.4) Parking turnoff (right). Excellent view of Navajo forms on every side. Note vegetation along the river, so characteristic of the Canyonlands region. Most apparent are cottonwood trees and the non-native, lacy tamarisk bush, picturesque but considered a pest because it crowds out native plants such as willows and because it utilizes much water.

2.7 (83.6) Parking turnoff (left) and informational sign calling attention to a prehistoric Indian storage granary in a cliff-niche across the river. Built about 800 years ago by Fremont Indians, it is typical of storage units designed to protect corn and other foods against rodents and insects.

3.6 (84.5) Parking turnoff (both sides) and wooded picnic area. Toilet, tables, no water. Delightful scenic surroundings.

Across the river, at the bend in the canyon but indistinct from here, Spring Canyon emerges from a maze of Navajo buttes in a narrow gateway. Spring Canyon is the park's longest and largest canyon, beginning on the slopes of Thousand Lake Mountain at more than 8,000 feet. See page 101 for hiking details.

4.4 (85.3) Parking turnoff at mouth of Grand Wash (right). Grand Wash Trail may be hiked in either of two directions: from this spot or from parking area on the South Park Drive. See page 89 for details. *Do not enter Grand Wash if a storm is threatening.*

The canyon has been used since pioneer days as a route for driving cattle and sheep. During turn-of-the-century years, it is said, Grand Wash and vicinity harbored Butch Cassidy and other outlaws.

5.8 (86.7) Elijah Cutler Behunin Cabin (right). Built of red sandstone, with one window, a door and fireplace, the rustic building was erected in 1892. Its roof is made of slabs and logs, covered with water-resistant bentonite clay. Cutler and his wife Jane were parents of 10 living children at the time this building was erected. They planned to add other rooms eventually. While living at this spot (2 years) the parents and youngest children slept in the house, older boys in a dugout, and girls in a wagon box.

The family worked energetically to divert the river, clear the valley bottom, plant fields and orchards. During

Behunin Cabin *Fran Barnes photo*

the third year violent floods washed everything away, as they did downstream at Aldridge and other settlements.

The Behunins were among the region's prominent early settlers, building the first house in Caineville about 1883. Cutler also was in charge of clearing the first road through Capitol Gorge.

6.2 (87.1) Parking turnoff (left) near the river. Here the Navajo is only about 100 feet high, having almost disappeared into the ground. Rising ahead is a sloping cliff of bedded Carmel formation.

About .2 mile ahead, to the right, is the former channel of Fremont River — abandoned when highway builders constructed a new channel to the left.

6.5 (87.4) Large parking turnoff (left). Abandoned river channel circles in from the right. Below the rim is a pool at the bottom of a steep rock slope, down which the Fremont River plunges in a picturesque waterfall. The pool and fall create a popular bathing spa during warmer months, when visitors and residents alike enjoy the cool water. *CAUTION: Serious injuries have resulted from sliding down the waterfall. Be safe! Keep off the rocks, which are slippery and dangerous when wet.*

Note the many strata beds in the cliff ahead, and their downward tilt.

Swimhole on Fremont River   *Ward Roylance photo*

7.4 (88.3) Small parking turnoff (left), on curve. In the sloping cliff ahead is an intriguing display of bedded rocks in the Carmel formation. A close inspection shows various types of siltstone, sandstone and claystone, in parallel layers. The Carmel was laid down in shallow seas and tidal flats, deposited on top of the desert-dune Navajo sandstone.

An especially vivid example of sediment removal and deposition is apparent along the upper rim of the tilted strata ahead. Note how the upper edges of the tilted Carmel have been planed off to a horizontal level, and a thick bed of boulders, sand and gravel laid down on top. It is likely that this erosion plane and deposition were the work of an ancient river, possibly occurring only some thousands of years ago.

The broad valley opening out to the north in this vicinity is known as South Desert. It was formed by erosion of younger, softer rocks along the Waterpocket Fold uplift's eastern slope. The valley continues north and west for about 20 miles, ending in the slopes of Thousand Lake Mountain. In its upper reaches are noble buttes and cliffs that resemble those of Cathedral Valley.

8.1 (89) Eastern boundary of Capitol Reef National Park.

8.4 (89.3) Parking and picnic area in a grove of cottonwood trees (right).

From here to Hanksville the road passes through Utah's colorful Painted Desert. It has left behind the sheer red cliffs and imposing dome-buttes of Capitol Reef. In their place are tiered ledges and fluted blue-gray mesas — "badlands" that affect the beholders in different ways. Many people consider this Painted Desert a masterpiece of natural art. Others — less familiar, perhaps, with desert esthetics — see only desolation. In this strange land, to a striking degree, beauty is truly in the eye of the beholder.

8.9 (89.8) Junction with road to Notom and Waterpocket Fold drive (right). See Road Log No. 4 for description.

Across the highway is a large parking area near the river, shaded by cottonwood trees, popular for picnicking and camping. The highway leaves South Desert and cuts through a high ridge comprised mostly of rainbow Morrison (dinosaur-age) rocks. The Morrison is a fruitful rockhound formation, being especially rich in agate, jasper, petrified wood, dinosaur bone, and colored quartz pebbles. Slopes are littered with volcanic boulders.

9.7 (90.6) Ruins of old rock dwelling across river to left. Years ago the river bottom for miles was utilized for crops, including sorghum cane.

10.7 (91.6) Parking turnoff to right (Moki Ruin). Picnic table. In a rock

60

crevice to the west is a small mud-brick structure "used by Fremont Indians about 900-1200 A.D. for the storage of food supplies. Stone doors were placed over the opening and sealed with mud to keep out rodents."

11.3 (92.2) Parking area and picnic table in a grove of trees (left). A short distance to the east, Pleasant Creek empties into the Fremont River. Pleasant Creek flows down from Boulder Mountain, passing through Sleeping Rainbow (Floral) Ranch and Notom enroute.

This is the site of old Aldridge, a farming hamlet or center of scattered farms. The area was settled in the 1880's, reaching a population peak during the 1890's. The climate was favorable and the soil fertile, producing bountiful crops such as melons, orchard fruits, vegetables, corn, alfalfa and sorghum cane, from which molasses was made.

Here, however, as elsewhere along the lower Fremont, it proved a heartbreaking task to obtain a reliable water supply for irrigation, even though water was plentiful. Most families had moved away by the turn of the century, many of them settling in other Wayne County communities.

11.7 (92.6) Junction (left) with River Ford road leading to Cathedral Valley and the park's North District. See Road Log No. 5 for details.

12.5 (93.4) Junction with road (right) leading to Notom, 4 miles. This is old U-24, used before the new highway was opened in 1962. About 2 miles toward Notom, the road passes through an outcropping of soft Dakota formation where fossilized oyster shells are abundant. The right-hand ridge offers (from its rim, accessible by short hike), a truly spectacular view of Capitol Reef's golden domes and slopes, rising above a foreground of Painted Desert slopes of Morrison clay. Pleasant Creek flows below, through an oasis valley.

The valley stretching north and south is formed in lower levels of the blue-gray Mancos formation, which was laid down in shallow, somewhat stagnant seas of the early Cretaceous period, about 100 million years ago. The Cretaceous was the final period when seas covered this land.

The Mancos forms the weird blue-gray ridges, slopes and grand fluted mesa walls in the Caineville and Henry Mountains vicinity. Its total thickness amounts to thousands of feet — thicker, in fact, than any other rock formations in the Capitol Reef area.

It is noteworthy that these barren but scenically dramatic clays, muds, shales and sandstones once covered the entire region, burying the older rocks — and themselves being buried by thousands of feet of even younger rocks. Since then the Cretaceous and younger rocks have been eroded away over most of the interior of Canyonlands, leaving an "island" of Cretaceous rocks in the Caineville-Henry Mountains area.

Waterpocket Fold stretches off to the south, its crest a jagged ridge of buttes and promontories.

14.1 (95)   Blue Dugway. The road here affords a stirring overview of Capitol Reef's majestic domes.

Those in the mood for a short hike to an unusual viewpoint should pull off the highway here (but *NEVER* when the ground is wet) and climb the low mudstone ridge to the right. The summit reveals a weird, corrugated land in every direction—a 360 degree sweep around the horizon. Especially choice is the eastern view across Mancos badlands and mesa-cliffs. Below, cottonwood-lined Sandy Creek flows toward a meeting with the Fremont.

15.1 (96)   Cross Fremont River.

15.6 (96.5) Old highway (right). Formerly the main highway between Caineville and towns to the west, this unpaved but exceptionally scenic road follows the Fremont River at the base of Caineville Reef. In dry weather, even a short drive through the river gate is worthwhile. The road is passable to Caineville (3 miles) in dry weather.

The area's tremendous wrinkled cliffs of Blue Gate shale (Mancos) are among the most awesome features of this country, from the Caineville mesas south to the Henrys.

As it approaches Caineville, the old road passes a log cabin (left), hidden behind lush vegetation growing along the canal. This rustic structure, the first house in Caineville, was built about 1882 by E.C. and Jane Behunin, the town's first settlers, who also built the rock house in Fremont River Canyon (see mile 5.8, this tour).

16.1 (97)   The main highway continues through blue-gray hills, with vistas of weird breaks opening to the north.

18.5 (99.4) Cross Caineville Wash. Normally dry, the wash drains a large expanse to the north and can become a torrent in wet weather.

18.6 (99.5) Road to the left gives access to the North District of Capitol Reef National Park (Cathedral Valley); also to public (BLM) grazing lands and scenic points outside the park. See Road Log No. 5.

18.9 (99.8) Old highway (right), leading along Caineville Reef and Fremont River. See description above. Behunin's log cabin, the first house in Caineville, is beside this road, about a mile from the highway.

19.1 (100)   CAINEVILLE (also known as Cainesville). Settled during the 1880's by Mormon farmers and stockraisers, Caineville has always been one of the most isolated communities in

Utah.

Water was the pioneers' main concern; though the river carried a plentiful supply, disastrous floods washed out their irrigation works and fields time after time.

In 1909 an especially terrible flood occurred, after which most people moved away — many of them to upper valley towns. Today a few families live in the community; others reside elsewhere, coming now and then to farm.

Local farms produce fine alfalfa, melons, corn and other crops. The old frame meetinghouse, dating from the 1890's, still stands. It was used also as a schoolhouse and community center.

Caineville Trading Post and Restaurant, on the highway, features Mexican food. Also available: groceries and supplies, handmade jewelry, rocks. Local produce in season.

CAINEVILLE TO HANKSVILLE (20 miles)

East of Caineville, U-24 follows the river through picturesque river valley and desert country known as Blue Valley.

The huge Caineville mesas dominate the scenery for the first 10 miles or so, along with the strange "moonscape" badlands at their feet. Five miles east of Caineville, Factory Butte comes into view north of the highway. This enormous "island" of Cretaceous rocks is almost a square mile in extent and rises 1,600 feet above a widespreading plain. It is one of the largest free-standing buttes in Utah.

Blue Valley, along the river east of Caineville, has witnessed several attempts at colonization, dating from the 1880's. For the first 30 years or so it flourished to a degree, the east end being named Giles in honor of Henry Giles, first Mormon bishop. But the temperamental river defeated the people here as it did most of those of Caineville. The ruins of an old rock house beside the highway remind today's travelers that a scattered community once existed in this forbidding land.

39   (120)   HANKSVILLE (eleva. 4,250 feet). Hanksville is a highway center at the junction of U-24 leading north to Green River, and U-95 leading to marinas on Lake Powell, to Natural Bridges National Monument, and to communities of southeastern Utah.

Long a quiet, isolated farming and ranching community, Hanksville is relatively thriving today. Rich uranium deposits are being mined nearby, and highway traffic provides an economic boost. The town bears little resemblance to the rustic village of 10 or 20 years ago.

Hanksville was settled in 1882 by Mormon pioneers

and named for Ebenezer Hanks, one of its founders and a cousin of Ephraim K. Hanks, settler of Floral Ranch in Capitol Reef National Park.

Services: Grocery stores, restaurants, service stations and garages, motels, rock shops, trailer parks. U.S. Bureau of Land Management area office.

North of Hanksville, U-24 follows San Rafael Reef to I-70 and Green River. Side roads lead west to Goblin Valley and San Rafael Swell, east to Robbers Roost and "The Maze" District of Canyonlands National Park.

South of Hanksville, U-95 crosses Burr Desert beneath peaks of the Henry Mountains. Side roads lead into the mountains and lower Fremont River canyons. At 26 miles the road forks, U-95 continuing to Lake Powell, Hite Marina and other points east; U-276 leading another 46 miles south to Bullfrog Resort and Marina.

This paved route from Hanksville to Bullfrog is exceptionally scenic. It may be combined with the Water-pocket Fold drive for an outstanding tour of 2 days or longer. See Road Log No. 4.

Bullfrog Resort and Marina (address Hanksville, Utah 84734) is the largest of three marinas at the north end of Lake Powell. The man-made lake occupies Glen Canyon of the former Colorado River and extends nearly 200 miles behind Glen Canyon Dam near the Arizona-Utah border. It is one of western America's most popular recreation sites, attracting several million visitors each year for boating, camping, exploring, fishing, sightseeing, etc.

Facilities and services at Bullfrog Resort-Marina include:
Motel accommodations/restaurant
Gasoline/auto and boat servicing
Campground (National Park Service)
Trailer and camper hookups
Groceries and supplies
Boat launching, docking, storage
Houseboat rentals
Boat and motor rentals
Airplane landing strip
Boat tours/fishing charters

Works of natural art "so suggestive of intelligence that it is difficult to persuade ourselves that the blind forces of nature could have achieved such a result."

Clarence E. Dutton

Navajo Dome *Ward Roylance photo*

Lake Powell *Ward Roylance photo*

Side canyon pool *NPS photo*

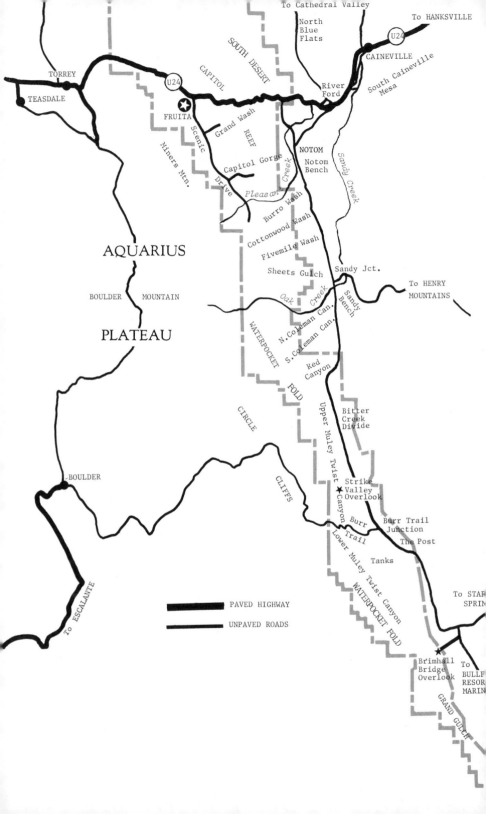

Descriptive Road Log
No. 4

EAST SIDE OF WATERPOCKET FOLD
South of Utah Highway 24
With loop extension from Burr Trail through Circle Cliffs to Boulder and Torrey

This exceptionally scenic route is an unpaved, fair-weather dirt road that leads south along the spectacular whaleback slope of the Waterpocket Fold's east side. It winds in a valley between the Fold on the west and the cliff-based Henry Mountains on the east, giving access to scenic points and hiking areas of the park's wild South District.

The road should not be driven in wet weather, when portions may become slick and muddy. Even in dry weather it may be rough and sandy in spots, but can normally be driven without difficulty in passenger cars.

Side roads lead east to the Henry Mountains, and west via Burr Trail through the Circle Cliffs to Boulder. The main road continues south to Lake Powell at Bullfrog Resort and Marina.

The road is mostly on public lands (U.S. Bureau of Land Management). At mile 20 it enters Capitol Reef National Park.

Miles from
Highway U-24

0.0 Junction U-24 and Waterpocket Fold road, 9 miles east of Park Visitor Center. Turn south on unpaved road marked "Notom." Road soon climbs out of Fremont River canyon on a steep dugway. Flats above give closeup views of Capitol Reef's splendid east-dipping slopes, its beautifully colored domes and crests. The Henry Mountains (north peaks) come into full view and will be landmarks from here southward.

THE HENRY MOUNTAINS
Standing as sentinel landmarks, visible from all over Utah's canyon country, the Henry Mountains are one of the Colorado Plateau's geologically unusual "island ranges." Scenically, if not

technically, they are a part of Capitol Reef National Park, inasmuch as their northern peaks, at least, can be seen from every section of the park.

Actually the Henry range consists of five distinct peaks. They are:

Mount Ellen - 11,615 feet elevation
Mount Pennell - 11,371 feet
Mount Hillers - 10,723 feet
Mount Holmes - 7,930 feet
Mount Ellsworth - 8,235 feet

Mount Ellen, the northern and by far the most massive peak, is joined to Mount Pennell by Penellen Pass. Together, these two peaks are the most striking landmarks on the park's eastern horizon. The other three peaks are normally not visible except from overlooks in the south.

The Henrys are unusual in several respects. Geologically, they are noted for their uncommon "laccolithic" structure, having been formed by the upwelling of igneous magma, or molten rock, which intruded into and pushed up the overlying sedimentary layers. Since then much of this igneous material has been exposed by erosion.

Geographically the Henrys were among the last important ranges in the lower 48 states to be named and placed on topographic maps. When first seen by Major Powell and his party of river explorers in 1869, they did not appear on any official map. Powell first termed them the "Unknown Mountains," afterwards naming them for Professor Joseph Henry, Secretary of the Smithsonian Institution at that time.

2.0 Cross Pleasant Creek, a small perennial stream flowing down from Boulder Mountain and cutting through Capitol Reef in a deep, very scenic canyon.

3.5 Junction with east road connecting Notom with U-24 (4 miles).

4.0 Notom Junction (5,200 feet eleva.). A cheerful oasis of huge cottonwood trees and green alfalfa fields, watered by Pleasant Creek, Notom was long a small ranching and farming center on the main road between Caineville and Fruita. In 1962 a new paved route (U-24) was opened in Fremont River canyon, bypassing Notom. Before then, U-24 passed through Notom and Capitol Gorge (see Log No. 1).

There is an impressive view from the fields south of Notom, west to Golden Throne and its companion domes, looming majestically above the gash of Capitol Gorge. (Golden Throne is the left-hand dome.) Boulder Mountain rises high beyond.

As it ascends Notom Bench, the road affords ever-changing panoramas of Waterpocket Fold to the west and the rugged breaks of South Caineville Reef to the east.

6.0 Notom Bench. An inconspicuous dirt sideroad (left) at 6.3 miles leads to the eastern edge of the bench and an overview of Utah's unearthly Painted Desert—a landscape so corrugated and colored with such an extraordinary range of unusual hues that it cannot be evaluated by ordinary standards of esthetics. The blue-gray, pleat-skirted Caineville mesas sprawl to the northeast, and beyond them the weird slopes of San Rafael Swell. Below the rim is a rainbow valley, leading upward to the grand escarpments that support the Henry Mountains.

6.4 Junction with Pleasant Creek road (right), giving access to the park boundary a short distance west. Pleasant Creek and Burro canyons yawn to the right, between exquisite sandstone slopes and buttes.

From the park boundary a non-maintained foot trail leads through Pleasant Creek Canyon to Sleeping Rainbow (Floral) Ranch at the south end of the main park road. See page 104 for hiking details.

For hikers who enjoy moderately strenuous slickrock walking and climbing, the open, gently undulating sandstone slopes between Pleasant Creek Canyon and Capitol Gorge offer one of the finest and most accessible slickrock hiking areas in the park.

6.8 Descend Notom Bench into the broad valley of Sandy Creek, which drains the country this side of Bitter Creek Divide and empties into Fremont River near Caineville. Panoramic views from this area are very impressive.

8.1 Burro Wash. Burro Wash and the next two washes south (Cottonwood and Fivemile) are small, usually dry streambeds that drain three deep box canyons in the slopes of the Fold. They offer popular day or overnight hikes of 3 to 5 miles each way, passing through exceptionally narrow gorges before opening into wider cliff-walled canyons. Wading may be necessary in places. Fairly steep: vertical rise of 1,000 feet or more from road to upper end of canyons, which head atop west-facing Capitol Reef. *Carry water.*

9.4 Cottonwood Wash, a sandy ravine containing scattered cottonwood trees. *See Burro Wash above.*

10.4 Fivemile Wash. A great Navajo dome and ridge mark the western skyline. *See Burro Wash above.* Wayne-Garfield county line. 5,100 feet elevation.

13.3 Sheets Wash. This large normally-dry wash drains Sheets Gulch, a splendid open gorge that has cut entirely through the main ridge of the Fold in a canyon more than 1,000 feet deep. Exceptionally scenic for hiking but without water. See page 105 for hiking possibilities.

Though one of the largest canyons in the park, even the mouth of Sheets Gulch is not visible from the road.

From viewpoints south of here, and from points on U-24 to the north, the ridge of grand white buttes looming above the

Gulch along its north rim is prominent on the skyline for many miles. The largest butte of all, having no official name, reaches an altitude of 7,200 feet, or 2,000 feet above the road.

14.1 Sandy Ranch junction. Left (east) fork gives access to the Henry Mountains, which tower 6,000 feet above the valley floor here. Mount Ellen is the largest peak, directly to the east. Cretaceous rocks are grandly impressive here, forming a tremendous ridge of terraced cliffs and buttes.

14.4 Oak Creek ford (normally shallow). An all-year stream, Oak Creek flows down from Boulder Mountain, where it is the source of several important reservoirs. In an airline distance of only 20 miles, Oak Creek descends from 11,000 feet at its head to 5,200 feet at its mouth. It provides irrigation water for Sandy Ranch, one of the area's major ranching operations.

Highly scenic Oak Creek Canyon is popular for overnight or long one-day hikes. See page 106 for hiking details.

From the ford, road climbs about 200 feet to Sandy Bench, also known as Sandy Creek Benches.

15.0 Sandy Bench affords a fine view of the sculptured wall of the Fold, dramatically broken here by Sheets Gulch and Oak Creek Canyon. Boulder Mountain rises against the western sky, and the great white ridge above Sheets Gulch becomes more visible.

To the south of Oak Creek Canyon, red-walled North and South Coleman canyons cut into the steep dip of the Fold, here 2,000 feet high. Behind narrow gates, these short box canyons widen out into cliff-sided amphitheaters, displaying in their walls all the colorful rocks that appear in the face of Capitol Reef. The canyons are scenic and may be hiked, but rock falls make for difficult going. The high red walls of Red Canyon are visible ahead, beneath a flat-top butte on the Fold's crest.

The east rim of Sandy Bench overlooks irrigated fields in the valley below, and above them majestic cliffs and buttes at the base of Mount Ellen.

17.5 Descend from Sandy Bench. Weaver Ranch is on the right, its fields watered from wells.

18.0 The flat-top butte atop the Fold, slightly ahead and to the right, is highest point (7,640 feet) in the park's South District. The road in this area is about 5,400 feet above sea level.

For some distance in this vicinity, the light-colored Navajo sandstone recedes downward from the Fold's whaleback, exposing reddish Kayenta rocks and massive red Wingate sandstone, the cliff former.

19.0 Entering the Narrows. Here the channel of Sandy Creek, followed by the road, narrows somewhat. On either side are interesting exposures of pastel, streaked sandstone, topped by many-layered Summerville formation, a picturesque evenly-bedded siltstone, mudstone and sandstone.

20.0 **Entering Capitol Reef National Park.** From this point on, the road is within park boundaries. Travelers are subject to park regulations respecting off-road vehicle travel, rock and fossil collecting, camping, hiking, etc.

The entire valley begins to narrow here as lofty Cretaceous cliffs on the east, painted in shades of blue-gray, green and buff, pinch closer to the Waterpocket Fold on the west. The scalloped upper edge of Tarantula Mesa rises high to the left, Cedar Mesa to the right.

22.2 Cedar Mesa Campground. Tables, toilet. No water. From the campground a trail follows an old mining road westward, leading finally to *Red Canyon* (barely visible to the northwest), an extraordinary, oval-shaped box canyon enclosed by sheer cliffs towering about a thousand feet above its floor. The canyon, a geological curiosity, is only about a mile in length and half a mile wide. It provides an exciting hike of 3 or 4 miles round trip. *Carry water.*

Southward, the road parallels a low ridge to the right. Short hikes to the crest of this ridge afford excellent views along the Fold.

25.8 Bitter Creek Divide (5,650 feet elevation), a low summit marking the drainage divide between Sandy Creek on the north (Fremont River) and Halls Creek on the south (Colorado River-Lake Powell).

From Bitter Creek Divide southward for several miles the road follows along Oyster Shell Reef, a well known fossil deposit that is now within the park. *No collecting permitted.* These "petrified" oysters were deposited in shallow seas of about 130 million years ago, in the Dakota formation. They occur on both sides of the road but are more plentiful on the east.

30.0 Short hikes to the crest of the low, jagged, uptilted ridge to the
to   right are rewarded with dramatic views of the full face of the
32.0 Fold in all its variegated color, erosional intricacy and physical grandeur. Here the marvelous Navajo sandstone has been sculptured into fascinating whirls, alcoves, caves, steep cliffs, gentle

Aerial view of Waterpocket Fold looking north from the Burr Trail area. *NPS photo*

slopes, gorges — in short, seemingly every design possible for massive rock.

An especially exciting view may be had from an old mining road turnoff at 32.0 miles. Here the impact of bright colors, combined with amazing rock tilting and erosional effects is overwhelming. Massive exposures of sculptured Navajo sandstone are exceptional here. *Mine diggings are dangerous. Keep out!*

In this area the road is bordered by colorful Painted Desert slopes of soft Morrison clay, painted in shades of greenish-gray with reddish bands. This clay, while good to look at, is impassable when even slightly wet.

The eastern park boundary follows the rim of Tarantula Mesa on the east (left) and Swap Mesa beyond it to the south.

33.0 Peek-a-boo Arch appears high on the Fold's crest ahead, at the upper end of Burr Trail. From points to the south, the arch resembles the eye in the horned head of a lizard or dinosaur, whose body drapes below along the slope of the Fold.

On the left, Tarantula Mesa is separated from Swap Mesa by a wide opening formed by Bitter Creek. Through this gap can be seen peaks of the Henrys.

33.9 Burr Trail Junction. See below (end of this log) for description of road leading west to Boulder.

The Burr Trail is visible to the west, climbing the steep flank of the Fold where it has been broken open, forming a natural passageway known as Burr Canyon.

South of here for several miles the slope of the Fold reaches a climax of erosional detail and vivid coloring. The Navajo sandstone, subtly tinted with gold, has been shaped into a maze of domes, cones, spires and myriad other remarkable forms. In the process, nature has created sheer-walled box canyons, hundreds of feet deep but short in length, exquisitely colored and contoured.

This area is popular for day hiking and rock climbing, with exceptional opportunities for personal exploration in a limited area of several square miles.

35.8 Hikers' parking area. Leave vehicles here while hiking the area described above.

Among the hiking possibilities here is Surprise Canyon: "a narrow, usually shaded gorge that can be hiked in 1 to 2 hours round trip. Practiced scramblers can go to the head of this canyon, cross over the divide, and come out the next canyon north."

36.3 The Post (sign) was formerly the site of a roundup corral and a cabin, now merely a reference location.

A connecting cutoff trail leads 2½ miles from parking area to Lower Muley Twist Canyon, affording hikers a shorter route choice than the full length of the canyon.

A short distance from The Post, turn right on spur road to corral and parking area (.6 mile). Southward, Halls Creek Valley (Grand Gulch) and Waterpocket Fold continue for about 30 miles to Lake Powell. At the corral is a parking and pickup area for hikers, including those walking the full length of Lower Muley Twist Canyon (5 miles south to the canyon mouth).

Within a few miles of this point are some of the largest waterpockets or tanks in the park. These include Willow and Cottonwood tanks, about a mile south of the parking area. Muley Tanks are about a mile or so below the mouth of Muley Twist Canyon. The water in these tanks—or at least some of the upper tanks—is suitable for drinking with treatment.

For several years during the 1880's Charles Hall operated a primitive ferry where Halls Creek joined the Colorado River in Glen Canyon. The ferry was used infrequently by travelers between older settlements west of the river and newly-settled Bluff in the southeast corner of the state. They entered or left Halls Creek Valley by way of Lower Muley Twist Canyon, the Circle Cliffs, and canyons of the Escalante River system.

Today the valley and Fold below this point are wilderness, visited by a few sturdy backpackers each year. Limited water is available in pockets and several springs, but the supply is neither dependable nor potable at times. *Persons intending to enter this area should confer and register, in advance, with park rangers.*

37.3 Boundary of Capitol Reef National Park. Enter U.S. Bureau of Land Management (public) lands. Road climbs out of Halls Creek Valley to bench lands above.

45.3 Junction with road leading left to Starr Spring (21 miles) on east side of the Henry Mountains. Continue south toward Bullfrog Marina, which is 22 miles from junction (67 miles from U-24). Views from this part of Big Thompson Mesa are outstandingly scenic, sweeping across an unearthly landscape of gorges and cliffs, buttes and standing rocks, stretching away in every direction. Looming above all are the bulky mass of Aquarius Plateau (Boulder Mountain) toward the northwest, the five peaks of Henry Mountains across the eastern horizon.

46.7 Junction with spur road leading right (west). Along this spur road 2½ miles to Halls Creek-Brimhall Bridge overlook. *Road is very rough. May not be suitable at times for passenger cars. Do not attempt in wet weather.*

From the overlook, several hundred feet above the floor of Grand Gulch (Halls Creek Valley), the Waterpocket Fold can be seen in its splendid ruggedness for miles to north and south. Directly across the valley, clearly visible in a Wingate sandstone canyon, is an unusual double-arch natural bridge. Known also as Wingate Arch, it bears the official name of Brimhall Natural Bridge, honoring the late Dr. Dean Brimhall of Fruita, prominent federal official and authority on the prehistoric Indian rock writings of Utah's remote canyon country. See Log No. 1 for more about Dr. Brimhall.

A 2½-mile trail winds down the cliffs to the valley floor and into the canyon below Brimhall Bridge; but a rock slide below the bridge makes access difficult and confusing for the average hiker. (Inquire at park headquarters before hiking to this bridge.)

In full view a short distance to the south is curious Red Slide, an enormous mud and rock flow which poured through a break in the Fold's crest, completely blocking the valley floor and forming a small lake at one time. The Red Slide probably was created during the most recent glacial period, only a few thousand years ago, when there was much more moisture than now. It carried rubble for several miles from the interior of Circle Cliffs, about 2,000 feet higher than the valley floor.

From below the overlook, a wilderness trail follows the valley floor southward about 10 miles to the park boundary, then about 7 miles farther to Lake Powell. *Do not enter this remote country without conferring and registering with park rangers.*

The side road continues south from the overlook for several miles, winding near the rim, but finally dead-ends at a spring. *Return to main Bullfrog Marina road.*

South for 21 miles through rugged and exceptionally scenic terrain to Bullfrog Resort & Marina on Bullfrog Bay of Lake Powell. See end of Road Log No. 3 for description.

Waterpocket Fold near Red Slide   *Ward Roylance photo*

WEST FROM BURR TRAIL JUNCTION TO CIRCLE CLIFFS AND BOULDER

33.9 Burr Trail Junction. Turn west here into Burr Canyon, a break in the face of Waterpocket Fold. The massive Navajo sandstone, which forms the main slope of the Fold elsewhere, has been completely removed here, leaving a great notch. Burr Trail climbs steeply up the underlying rocks in a series of switchbacks that rise some 800 feet in half a mile of horizontal distance. The route has been used by stockmen since later years of the 1900's.

On both sides, the trail affords an excellent cross-section look at the Fold's angle of slope. In this vicinity the Navajo sandstone is 1,000 feet thick, the Kayenta below is 300 feet, and the cliff-forming Wingate is more than 200 feet thick.

From top of the Burr Trail, the view eastward is superlative. It is said that the trail, canyon and an extensive rangeland known as Burr Desert, near Hanksville, were named for John Burr, an early-day stockman.

35.9 Parking area and hiker register for LOWER MULEY TWIST CANYON. A remarkable gorge that has been cut into the crest of the Waterpocket Fold, parallel to the Fold's north-south direction, the canyon winds tortuously for 12 miles before exiting into Halls Creek Canyon (Grand Gulch). See page 106 for hiking description.

37.0 Junction with road (right) giving access to UPPER MULEY TWIST CANYON and STRIKE VALLEY OVERLOOK. Recommended only for 4-wheel-drive vehicles beyond the first half mile, though others with high clearance might be able to negotiate the sandy wash and rocky ledges with difficulty.

At .4 mile is a park register and hikers parking area. Peek-a-boo Arch looms overhead. The road enters narrow Muley Twist Canyon, confined between white Navajo slopes and cliffs on the right (east), Kayenta/Wingate cliffs and ledges on the left. Rocks are eroded into fantastic shapes and patterns, including a number of natural arches. One of these, on the west wall near the road, is an unusual double arch.

At 2.9 miles the road ends at a parking area. Ahead, a hiking trail leads along the canyon floor for another 6½ miles, through very scenic terrain. See page 106 for hiking details.

Right from the parking area, a marked trail leads several hundred yards through fine sand and across slickrock slopes to Strike Valley Overlook. From this superlative point atop the Fold's crest, the eye is met by a geologic spectacle of the first order. The floor of Halls Creek Valley lies a thousand feet below, formed along the crumbling edges of layer upon layer of uptilted strata. The valley is known as a "strike valley" because it parallels the "strike" or direction of axis of the Waterpocket Fold monocline.

The varicolored formations of sandstone, mudstone, siltstone before the viewer were laid down over millions of years, in a marvelous variety of environments such as oceans, lakes, tidal plains, swamps, deserts, rivers and deltas. Total thickness of strata exposed in the valley floor and cliffs to either side amounts to thousands of feet. And this is only what remains! As much as 7,000 feet, more or less, of younger rocks were laid down on top of the highest cliffs in the region — and even the Henrys themselves. They have all disappeared during the millions of years since deposition.

The Fold's steep, tilting, whaleback slope is visible in awesome overall dimension from here. On the east, tier upon tier of blue-gray, greenish and brownish cliffs rise toward peaks of the Henrys. These are of younger, less resistant Cretaceous age, reminders of a long-lasting ocean that once covered much of western America.

Most of the rock strata in view from the Strike Valley Overlook were tilted upward towards the west by the great crustal flexure that created the Waterpocket Fold monocline about 60 or 70 million years ago. Since then the Henry Mountains were formed by upward intrusion of volcanic magma into overlying sedimentary beds. See Geology chapter.

Return to main road. Continue toward Boulder.

38.7 Park picnic area (right).

39.2 West boundary of Capitol Reef National Park. This point is within the Circle Cliffs uplift, a great oval arena formed by an encircling ring of high cliffs.

Eastward, the view is a panorama of the jagged, vividly colored inner rampart of the hollowed-out uplift (actually the west side of the Waterpocket Fold). Exposed strata are similar to the rocks and scenery of Capitol Reef to the north.

Beyond the Circle Cliffs, the view encompasses all 5 peaks of the Henry Mountains and the grand terraced platforms upon which they stand. It is a truly awesome sight—one of the Plateau region's choicest scenes. Far off, indistinct in the distance, buttes and cliffs of Glen Canyon's red world lend a final accent of mystery and wonder to the view.

* * * * *

Westward, the road continues to Boulder, Escalante or Torrey. For most of the distance to Boulder it passes through public lands administered by the Bureau of Land Management. It is an excellent unpaved road maintained by Garfield County, though weather may affect its condition at times.

Rocks at the base of the encircling Wingate cliffs are unusually rich in petrified wood. Formerly, petrified logs of great size were common, but much easily collectible wood has been removed. *Collectors on public lands are limited in the quantity they may remove. Check with BLM for detailed regulations.*

40.9 Junction with road to left (south), leading to "Petrified Wood Area." This is a 16-mile loop road, giving access to a colorful but remote and rugged area in the vicinity of Wolverine Canyon, where petrified wood is relatively abundant. The road rejoins the main Boulder road near Long Canyon, 11 miles west.

Wolverine Canyon is one among a maze of short, deep, very picturesque canyons that drain the larger part of the Circle Cliffs basin into the lower Escalante River. Vehicles with 4-wheel-drive may penetrate into portions of this rugged area, but most of it remains accessible only by foot or on horseback.

The main road here traverses a summit of sorts at 6,800 feet. Wagon Box Mesa (7,300 feet) looms up to the south. The area is densely wooded with pygmy evergreens of uncommonly large size. Not far beyond the Wolverine turnoff, the road passes between Studhorse Peaks (low ridges used by wild stallions as lookout points), then enters the widespreading expanse of White Canyon Flat. A long line of great red cliffs forms the horizon ahead; Boulder Mountain rises above them, dark and massive.

45.7 Junction with road (right) leading to the Lampstand, 5 miles, an unusual butte in the broken country to the north.

48.2 Junction with road (right) also leading to the Lampstand, 5 miles.

51.6 Junction with road (left) leading south to Petrified Wood Area, 12 miles. This road is the west end of loop giving access to the Wolverine slopes, described above under 40.9 mileage reading.

Here the main road has left the open flats and is now beneath a red wall of lofty Wingate cliffs, rising above a colorful base of Chinle and Moenkopi rocks — similar to those in the face of Capitol Reef.

53.0 Entering upper Long Canyon, the road's route for the next 7 miles. The Diadem, a picturesque fluted ridge, crowns the cliff ahead.

53.5 Long Canyon Viewpoint (left, beneath the Diadem) overlooks much of the inner heart of the Circle Cliffs uplift — a tremendous sweep of rainbow colors and rocky grandeur.

From here the road follows the bottom of narrow Long Canyon, between sheer Wingate walls towering hundreds of feet above. The Wingate here is highly fractured in places, and some of it has been bleached to a whitish shade in contrast to its normal dark red (probably as a result of water leaching). The cliffs display intriguing erosional patterns and beautiful tonal designs effected by desert varnish.

60.0 Leave Long Canyon at its confluence with The Gulch, a sister gorge, and climb out onto the lower slopes of Boulder Mountain. The country here is open once more, characterized now by rounded domes, ledges and slopes of light-colored Navajo sandstone.

71.0 BOULDER and junction with State Highway U-12. Turn left to Escalante, 32 miles; or right to Anasazi Indian Village (1 mile) and Torrey (40 miles). See Road Log No. 2 for Boulder Mountain scenic drive and description of Anasazi Village.

Descriptive Road Log
No. 5

CATHEDRAL VALLEY
and Northern Waterpocket Fold

Waterpocket Fold emerges from Thousand Lake Mountain in a tremendous flow of ridge upon ridge of tilted, varicolored rock strata. From the mountain's eastern heights the Fold can be traced in its incredible complexity, from its emergence beneath one's feet until it becomes lost in hazy distance to the south.

The park's North District includes some of the fantastic high country where the Fold emerges from Thousand Lake Mountain, as well as part of the strange lower deserts known by such names as Cathedral Valley, South Desert and Middle Desert.

This country has been used for livestock grazing since settlers came to the nearby valleys a hundred years ago. In that sense it is hardly remote or unknown. Few stockmen are travel writers, however, and it was not until the mid-1940's that its scenic possibilities became known.

Only in recent years have roads been improved to passenger car level. Even now they are rough, rocky and sandy in spots — and in wet weather they are impassable. In winter the lower roads are usually dry but the route over Thousand Lake Mountain from Fremont is closed by snow.

CATHEDRAL VALLEY

The general area known as Cathedral Valley embraces an extremely rugged country between Thousand Lake Mountain and the Caineville mesas. Despite its beauty it remains one of the least known parts of Utah.

The "valley" consists of more than 50 miles of exquisitely carved Entrada cliffs, winding around in a labyrinth of ridges, mesas, alcoves, basins and valleys. Standing apart from these stately ramparts as eroded islands are buttes that resemble idealized cathedrals or temples.

These cliffs and buttes are majestic in size. So far as known, they

79

are truly unique in sculptural design. Esthetically they rank in a class by themselves.

Here the Gothic arch and vertical lines combine in an endless flow of elegant, upward-sweeping, three-dimensional forms. These arched and fluted forms are graceful and noble in the ultimate sense, with symmetry and harmony that approach the divine ideal. Emotion and a touch of mysticism are indispensable in fully appreciating the art of Cathedral Valley.

ROAD DESCRIPTIONS AND MILEAGE LOGS

(Mileages along roads *do not* allow for side trips to overlooks.) Carry drinking water. There are no improved campgrounds except on Thousand Lake Mountain (Elkhorn Forest Campground, Fishlake National Forest). Refer to equipment checklist on the inside back cover to make sure you are prepared. *Do not attempt in wet or threatening weather.* The road can be negotiated by passenger cars, keeping in mind that it is a dirt road, rough in places, and sandy in spots.

The central core of "cathedral" cliffs and buttes measures nearly 100 square miles in area. To reach this center it is necessary to drive many miles on rough roads. However, the access routes pass through outstandingly scenic terrain.

Visitors using the access roads from Highway U-24 may enter either at River Ford (mile 0.0 below) or at Caineville. If entry is made at Caineville, begin the log with mile 49.

Mileage reading

0.0 **River Ford Road** (Highway U-24/River Ford to Cathedral Junction - 28 miles)

This route involves a shallow ford across the Fremont River, at a point 11½ miles east of the Park Visitor Center. (U-24 milepost reading: 92.6). Take note of your car's odometer reading for reference.

Here, near the site of old Aldridge, the Fremont River flows through a wide valley. The ford provides a hard bottom and the water is usually no more than a foot deep; in flood, however, it may be deeper. If in doubt, take off your shoes and wade the stream to check.

The road winds through several areas of colorful Painted Desert hills of Morrison Brushy Basin clay, also known as Bentonite Hills. While this formation is picturesque, it makes the road impassable when wet, even with 4-wheel drive.

The road also passes across an extensive valley known as North Blue Flats which affords a sweeping panorama of the Waterpocket Fold from its meeting with Thousand Lake Mountain, south to the Henrys. This area—in fact, much of the entire region—has been used as a grazing ground since pioneer days, but there is little apparent forage along the road here.

12.0 Junction with road leading left (west) to **Lower South Desert Overlook** (1 mile). This high point affords a stirring view down into South Desert, a wide valley between the corrugated slope of Waterpocket Fold and the high cliff on which the point is located. The Fold's dramatic sculpturing and deformed rock layers are very impressive from here. Near the overlook are majestic cathedral buttes, the largest of which is known variously as the Jail House or Court House.

14.0 **Entering Capitol Reef National Park.** Vehicles restricted to maintained roads. No collecting of rocks, plants, artifacts, etc.

17.0 **Ackland Spring** is not suitable for human use (do not drink!); however, it is an important supply for cattle. Surrounding it is a rugged maze of low cliffs and shallow canyons known as The Hartnet. Upper Hartnet Draw drains this country into Caineville Wash.

23.5 At the top of a ridge is junction (left) with road leading 0.2 miles to **South Desert Overlook.** Here, from the edge of a dizzy cliff, South Desert valley is in full view. Wonderful erosional forms are on its floor, on the cliff face, and on the incredible slopes of Waterpocket Fold — which melds in this vicinity with the massive bulk of Thousand Lake Mountain. The total effect of all is a symphony of natural grandeur, one of the choicest views in Utah.

Accenting the scene are several remarkable volcanic intrusions or plugs which forced a path through sedimentary rocks, then solidified. One of these is only a hundred feet or so from the overlook point, permitting close examination of how the native rock was changed by igneous heat.

23.7 Only 0.2 mile from the turnoff to South Desert Overlook is another, leading right 0.4 to **Cathedral Valley Overlook.** A short walk from the parking area brings into view some of the park's more remarkable buttes, ridges and cliffs — all part of a great erosional system that begins high up on the mountain's shoulder as a huge amphitheater and extends eastward for many miles.

The amphitheater's west wall is 2,000 feet high. Though not as vivid or varied in coloring as the amphitheater at Cedar Breaks, it does resemble Cedar Breaks in grandness of scale and architecture.

The basin immediately below the rim is Upper Cathedral Valley, also known as West Cathedral Valley. Its cliffs and buttes are 300 to 400 feet high, of reddish-brown Entrada formation.

(The Entrada, it should be noted here, has peculiar characteristics. In places it is a massive sandstone with few discernible layers, formed in desert dunes — as in Arches National Park. Elsewhere it might be a water-laid sandstone or siltstone, as in this area, where it consists of numerous layers of alternating sandstone and softer rocks. These hard-and-soft layers are responsible for Cathedral Valley's unique erosional patterns.)

24.0 **Major junction.** The road straight ahead leads to Thousand Lake Mountain and Fremont. See Road Description   below for details of this mountain route (Fremont to Cathedral Valley).

The right-hand road descends in steep switchbacks to the valley floor. Off to the left (0.2 mile) is a small "line cabin" and corral built years ago by cattlemen who have used this country as grazing range since early days of settlement. The road passes near a group of superb cathedrals (left), irresistible models for visitors with cameras, incomparable examples of nature's erosional artistry.

As the road turns east, a ridge on the right exhibits three conelike spires bearing the names Ma, Pa and Little Henry. The ridge is known today as Walls of Jericho.

28.0 **CATHEDRAL JUNCTION.** The road straight ahead continues through Middle Desert to East Cathedral Valley and U-24 at Caineville (20 miles). See description immediately below. The left-hand road leads north to Baker Ranch and a junction with Interstate 70/State Highway 10 (24 miles). From all these roads, forks give access to remote slopes of the San Rafael Swell. A striking butte known as Solomon's Temple can be viewed from the road 4 miles north of Cathedral Junction, near the park's northern boundary.

Middle Desert Road   Cathedral Junction to U-24/
Caineville - 21 miles.

Take special note of the remarkable lava ridge or dike a few yards to the north. Dikes are common in this area and are explained below. This particular group was called the **Walls of Jericho** by Charles Kelly in his pioneer magazine article on the region.

Other points of interest seen from this road include miles of cathedral cliffs, Gypsum Sinkhole, Glass Mountain, Temples of the Sun and Moon (highest monoliths in the park's North District), Black Mountain and numerous volcanic intrusions. For most of the distance, this road is on BLM land; however, points of interest such as Gypsum Sinkhole and Temples of the Sun and Moon are within the park.

29.0 Side road (right) leading 1.2 miles to **Gypsum Sinkhole.** This most curious phenomenon is a cylindrical pit at the base of a cliff, measuring about 80 feet in depth and perhaps 50 feet in diameter. Its age and origin are unknown. Formerly it was believed to have been caused by a meteor, but evidence does not support this theory. A more likely explanation involves the solution and carrying away of gypsum by water; this explanation, however, does not answer certain questions. Whatever the pit's origin, it is an intriguing and impressive point of interest. *Danger: Keep back from the rim!*

Above the road near the pit is a fascinating example of an *igneous dike,* or vertical intrusion of lava. Originally the black lava was embedded in sedimentary rocks, but these have eroded away from much of the dike, completely exposing it in places. Such igneous intrusions are very apparent along the main road for some miles. They are among the most remarkable geological aspects of the Park's North District and deserve careful attention.

Dikes were formed by the upwelling of lava into cracks or fissures in the native rock. As noted, such intrusions (or variations known as plugs) occur in South Desert and near South Desert Overlook; at Cathedral Junction (Walls of Jericho); and near Gypsum Sinkhole. Other examples can be seen from the road between Cathedral Junction and Temples of the Sun and Moon.

Lava also intruded horizontally between sedimentary rock beds. These horizontal intrusions are known as *sills.* **Black Mountain** — prominently visible to the east — is a very dramatic example of this horizontal type of intrusion. Note how it exhibits a number of different beds or layers of alternating lava and sedimentary rock, resulting in a "sandwich" effect. On a smaller scale, there is a similar exposure of interbedding close to the road several miles east of Cathedral Junction.

(If the lava had not interbedded evenly, but rather had pushed up the overlying rock in a dome, an igneous "laccolite" would be the result. That type of volcanic activity created the Henry Mountains.)

An even more extensive area of igneous intrusion is located about 10 miles to the northeast, on the slopes of San Rafael Swell. Undoubtedly the area's igneous activity is all a result of stresses created by the Swell, the Waterpocket Fold, plateau uplifts, and other deformations of earth's crust in this vicinity.

36.0 A road leads right into a valley containing **Temple of the Sun, Temple of the Moon, and Glass Mountain.** This short but sandy road may cause difficulty, particularly where it climbs out of the wash. Caution!

The temples are splendid freestanding monoliths, often pictured in travel articles and probably the Valley's best known attractions.

Temple of the Sun rises several hundred feet above its base, its sides almost sheer. Temple of the Moon is slightly smaller.

A short distance from Temple of the Sun is Glass Mountain, an impressive mound of selenite crystals. Selenite somewhat resembles mica but is a form of gypsum. Here its large blocky crystals are intermingled in a complex mass. *No collecting!*

The remaining 13 miles to U-24 at Caineville pass through increasingly broken country. There are beautiful exposures of Painted Desert slopes, rugged ledges and canyons. The majestic Caineville mesas come close and Waterpocket Fold stretches off

Upper Cathedral Valley   *NPS photo*

into the southern distance. The Henrys are prominent as always, and the dark plateaus. Everywhere around is a seemingly chaotic jumble of rocky wilderness — a landscape that could accurately be termed unearthly.

49.0 Junction with Highway U-24 at Caineville.

See Road Log No. 3 for description of U-24 between Visitor Center and Caineville-Hanksville.

Fremont to Cathedral Valley via Thousand Lake Mountain

This alternate approach to Cathedral Valley offers advantages of alpine scenery, cool forests, and lofty vantage points for viewing the Cathedral Valley country from above. One drawback is that the mountain road is open only during warmer months — perhaps mid-May to late October. Make local inquiry if in doubt. Good sources: Park rangers, Visitor Center, or Fishlake National Forest in Loa and Richfield.

Distance from Fremont to Upper (West) Cathedral Valley is about 20 miles, 15 miles of which is unpaved mountain road — some of it steep, rocky and rough. The road climbs from Fremont at 7,000 feet elevation to a high pass at 9,500 feet, then descends the east slope of Thousand Lake Mountain. Cathedral Valley has an elevation of about 6,000 feet.

Views from the mountain are among the grandest in Utah, encompassing a vast sweep of painted desert—a truly unique landscape having no counterpart.

Elkhorn Campgroud (Fishlake National Forest) is on Thousand Lake Mountain only 3 miles from the access road and 8 miles from Cathedral Valley itself.

Monoliths in Cathedral Valley   *Fran Barnes photo*

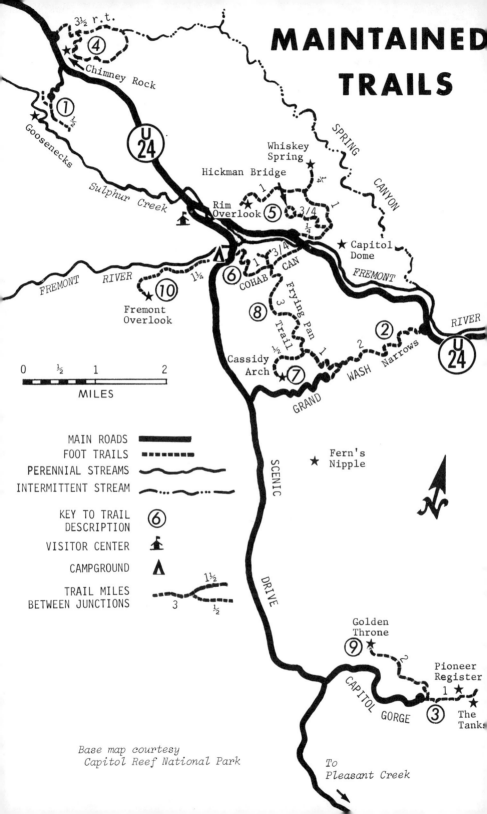

MAINTAINED TRAILS

3½ r.t.
④
Chimney Rock

①
½
Goosenecks

U24

Sulphur Creek

SPRING CANYON

Whiskey Spring
★
4/7

Hickman Bridge
1

Rim Overlook
★
⑤
3/4
1
1/4

Capitol Dome
★

FREMONT

FREMONT RIVER
1¼
⑩
★
Fremont Overlook

⑥
COHAB
1
3/4
CAN

⑧
Frying Pan
3
Trail
1

②
WASH Narrows
2

RIVER
U24

Cassidy Arch
★
½
⑦
1
GRAND

Fern's Nipple
★

N

0 ½ 1 2
MILES

MAIN ROADS ▬▬▬▬▬
FOOT TRAILS ▬ ▬ ▬ ▬
PERENNIAL STREAMS 〜〜〜
INTERMITTENT STREAM 〜·〜·〜

KEY TO TRAIL DESCRIPTION ⑥
VISITOR CENTER ⛪
CAMPGROUND ▲

TRAIL MILES BETWEEN JUNCTIONS
1½
3
½

SCENIC

DRIVE

Golden Throne
★
⑨
2

Pioneer Register
★
1
★
③
The Tanks

CAPITOL GORGE

Base map courtesy
Capitol Reef National Park

To Pleasant Creek

HIKING IN THE PARK

For those who like to explore on foot, Capitol Reef National Park offers myriad opportunities for hiking, scrambling and rock climbing.

Marked routes near the Visitor Center provide access to matchless gorges, slickrock slopes, and dizzy cliff-top overlooks. These trails range from easy to strenuous, enabling almost everybody to experience the incomparable "feel" of smooth, solid rock underfoot...the cool shade of a cloistered canyon...the exhilaration of communing even for an hour or two with Mother Earth in its most primeval aspect.

Those with more time and endurance will find that the park's unbelievably rugged backcountry affords a great range of hiking choices with respect to terrain and possible routes. These opportunities are described in Part 2 of this chapter (page 97).

THE MAINTAINED TRAILS

An ever-growing number of people have come to realize that if they want to fully "experience" a place in more than a superficial way, they must walk.

Walking brings one close to the earth, physically, emotionally and spiritually. The walker sees, hears and "senses" things that escape the car-bound tourist: things such as subtle rock patterns...plants in their infinite detail...the sudden scurry of a tiny lizard...the sound of a bird, a rustling leaf, dripping water.

Or a walker might sit quietly among the age-old rocks, just feeling that haunting aura of eternity that so pervades the canyon country atmosphere.

Within a 10-mile radius of the Visitor Center are a number of maintained trails that provide an intimate acquaintance with Capitol

Reef's rainbow cliffs, profound canyons, and fantastic erosional forms. These trails are marked with signs, rock cairns and painted footprints. They are safe for prudent people. All are suitable for hikers in good physical condition, and some may be suitable—at least in part—for the elderly or handicapped. If in doubt, inquire at the Visitor Center or from a park ranger.

Be sure to read the Cautions, Regulations and Suggestions for Hikers at the end of this chapter!

WATER: Always carry drinking water if you intend to be away from your car for more than an hour. In hot weather, it is advisable to carry at least a pint of water per person per hour.

HIKING TIME: In estimating time, figure that *one mile of trail* will require *one hour of hiking time.* Fast walkers may reduce this time somewhat.

Easy and Fairly Easy Trails

Map Key

1 GOOSENECKS TRAIL

Length one way - 1/10 to 1/2 mile
Parking area - 1 mile from Highway U-24 (turnoff is 2.7 miles northwest of Visitor Center)

A short switchback trail leads from the parking area to the rim of Sulphur Creek Gorge, about 500 precipitous feet above the floor of the narrow canyon. Cut into the Miner's Mountain uplift, the gorge takes a sinuous path here; hence the name Goosenecks.

The thrilling view extends not only downward, but west to Torrey Knoll and Thousand Lake Mountain, and east along the main face of Capitol Reef.

Here, and in the canyon of Fremont River to the south, can be seen the oldest rocks exposed to view in the park: the light-colored Kaibab limestone and Coconino sandstone of Permian age (about 240 million years ago). These rocks, which are buried most deeply at Capitol Reef, are the uppermost rocks at Grand Canyon. In other words, many of the rock types at Capitol Reef today may once have covered Grand Canyon but have been eroded away from that area.

From the parking area a longer trail leads ½ mile along the canyon rim toward the east, affording choice views into the gorge and along the Reef's face.

There is no excellent beauty that hath not some strangeness in the proportion.

Francis Bacon

Grand Wash *NPS photo*

2 GRAND WASH TRAIL

Length one way - Up to 2.2 miles
Parking area - In Grand Wash, 4.7
miles from Visitor Center

(*Caution!* Do not enter Grand Wash in wet or threatening weather.)

The sandy trail follows along the bottom of Grand Wash, also known as Grand Gorge because of its imposing depth combined with an exceptionally narrow stream channel. Almost vertical cliffs form the canyon's walls, gradually pinching together until, in The Narrows (1.3 mile), they are about 500 feet high and only 20 feet apart. Full length of the trail between parking area and mouth of the wash at Highway U-24 is 2.2 miles. Hikers who wish to hike one way through the wash should arrange for pickup at the highway parking area.

Grand Wash has been used since pioneer days as a route for livestock drives. Also, according to local legend, it served as a travel route and hideout for Butch Cassidy, Silver Tip and other outlaws of the late 19th century, whose main hideout was in Robbers Roost to the east. Remains of an old log lean-to, supposedly built by outlaws but now collapsed and burned, can be seen at the upper end of the first tributary canyon on the left beyond the parking area.

Bear Canyon, an exceptionally scenic side gorge (first canyon below the parking area on the right) affords hiking access to Fern's Nipple and the broken heights of the Reef; inquire at Visitor Center.

About ¼ mile beyond the parking area, the Cassidy Arch-Frying Pan-Cohab Canyon Trail (see No. 7 below) leaves Grand Wash Trail and winds up the cliff on the left.

89

3 CAPITOL GORGE TRAIL Length one way - 1 mile
Parking area - 10.3 miles from
Visitor Center

(Caution! Do not enter Capitol Gorge in wet or threatening weather.)

From the parking area, the trail leads along the streambed between high sheer walls of Capitol Gorge. The cliffs tower hundreds of feet overhead, and in places are only 20 or 30 feet apart. It is hard to believe that for 80 years until 1962 this narrow, serpentine gorge was the main route of travel between west and east in this part of Utah.

Along the one-mile trail are examples of ancient Fremont Indian rock art, dating from 700 or 800 years ago. More recently, white travelers added their names and dates on a part of the cliff known as Pioneer Register. The earliest date shown is 1871. Many of those who left their names were pioneers of the region. *Needless to say, Do Not deface the writings or mark the cliffs!*

The trail ends at a small side canyon which contains potholes known as The Tanks. Formerly these contained a long-lasting supply of water, resulting from rainfall, but the lower tanks are normally dry today. They typify the countless hollowed-out "waterpockets" so common along the Waterpocket Fold, and the basis for its name.

More energetic walkers may wish to hike an additional 3 miles to Notom, for prearranged pickup.

Golden Throne Trail (see No. 9 below) climbs up the left-hand wall of the gorge from the parking area.

Fairly Strenuous and Strenuous Trails

4 CHIMNEY ROCK TRAIL Length - 3½ miles round trip
(Fairly strenuous) Parking area - 3.2 miles northwest of Visitor Center on Highway U-24

The fairly strenuous trail climbs steeply from 6,100 feet at the parking area to a high ridge at 6,640 feet, overlooking Chimney Rock. Enroute the trail affords superb high-level views of the Reef's face stretching off in colorful grandeur for many miles to left and right. During its course the trail zigzags up and down, winds along a lofty rim, follows the base of towering Wingate cliffs. Petrified wood fragments are abundant *(no collecting!)*.

A side route takes off from the main trail about one mile through Chimney Rock Canyon from the parking area, leading another eight miles to the lower reaches of Spring Canyon, exiting finally at the Fremont River and U-24 at a point 3.7 miles east of the Visitor Center. See page 102 for description of this very scenic route.

Hickman Natural Bridge   *Fran Barnes photo*

5 HICKMAN NATURAL BRIDGE - WHISKEY SPRING - RIM OVERLOOK TRAIL
(Fairly strenuous to strenuous)

Length one way - 1 mile to Hickman Bridge, 1½ mile to Whiskey Spring, 2¼ miles to Rim Overlook (about 3 miles if Hickman Bridge is visited)

Parking area - 1.9 miles east of Visitor Center on Highway U-24

This trail may be hiked in its entirety or in segments. A self-guiding booklet is available at trailhead for the Bridge segment.

Leaving the parking area, the trail follows the left bank of the river for a few hundred feet, then climbs to a terrace at the base of giant, beautifully sculptured Navajo sandstone cliffs, domes and buttes. Navajo Dome and Walker Peak loom overhead to the north; Capitol Dome is on the east.

About ¼ mile from the parking area, the trail forks: left to Hickman Natural Bridge (¾ mile), right to Whiskey Spring (1¾ mile) and Rim Overlook (2 miles).

The Bridge Trail (fairly strenuous) descends into a shallow, sandy-bottomed canyon which provides welcome shade on sunny days. The picturesque bridge comes into view at the end of this

91

canyon. As you climb out of the canyon, about ¼ mile from the bridge, watch for a storage cyst built about 800 years ago by Fremont Indians.

The bridge is a majestic natural span arching over a rocky watercourse. Named for Joseph Hickman, local educator who played a leading role in the establishment of Capitol Reef National Monument during the 1930's, it was known in earlier days as Broad Arch and Fruita Natural Bridge. Its setting is awesome; however, the bridge is difficult to photograph in its entirety without a wide-angle lens. The bridge measures 133 feet from rim to rim, more than 125 feet above the streambed.

Whiskey Spring, a seep at the end of a short canyon, was named because former-day moonshiners used the site for a whiskey still (water is supposed to have been more plentiful then). Walker Peak, a tremendous butte-form, towers to the right, its base a splendid cliff of fractured Navajo sandstone. The butte was named for Chief Walker (Wakara), a prominent Ute chief of pioneer days.

The Rim Overlook trail (strenuous) continues beyond Whiskey Spring turnoff, ascending the steep incline of the Fold. Views are indescribably grand: down into the white labyrinth of Fremont River Canyon...south along the crest of Capitol Reef with its wondrous tangle of intricately carved sandstone forms. Finally the trail ends at a breathtaking rim-edge point overlooking Fruita and the Visitor Center, a thousand feet below. Beyond them the view encompasses Miner's Mountain, gashed by the gorges of Fremont River and Sulphur Creek, and the face of the Reef winding away toward Torrey. *Be careful! Keep back from the rim!* Hikers may continue on to Longleaf Flat, a short distance to the right, where local residents used to graze their cattle. This is an exceptionally scenic area of picturesque Reef-top fins and cliffs.

6 COHAB CANYON TRAIL
(Fairly strenuous first ¼ mile of switchbacks)

Length one way - 1¾ mile
Trail may be entered from either end: West - across the road from campground. East - across U-24 from Hickman Bridge parking area

Cohab Canyon is a short, narrow, charming canyon that has been eroded into the upper edge of Capitol Reef. Legend has it that the canyon was used as a hiding place during the 1880's, by Mormon polygamists ("cohabitationists") when pursued by federal marshals. Its sculptured walls, broken by extremely narrow joint canyons, are carved into amazingly intricate designs.

Beyond Cohab Canyon on the east, the trail descends gradually to Fremont River Canyon and the highway. A side trail leads to the rim of the river gorge, where two overlooks provide spectacular views.

7 CASSIDY ARCH TRAIL
(Strenuous)

Length one way - 1¾ mile
Parking area - In Grand Wash, 4.7 miles south of Visitor Center

A rather strenuous but exceptionally scenic hike, the trail switchbacks up the north wall of Grand Wash, climbing nearly 1,000 feet between the parking area and Cassidy Arch. Most of the vertical distance is covered in the first half mile of trail; the remainder is moderate up-and-down travel along the base of cliffs, over ledges and slickrock slopes.

As with other trails, pinyon pine and juniper evergreens, shrubs and flowers add a pleasant accent to the multicolored rocks. Marvelous erosional forms are everywhere — above, below and all around. As the trail climbs higher, views into the abyss of Grand Wash become more thrilling. Higher points offer truly sublime panoramas. The trail's last half-mile or so is over undulating slickrock. (Note: Slickrock is not really very slick on moderate slopes but can be dangerous on steep dips, or when wet.)

Cassidy Arch was named for the outlaw Butch Cassidy, a native of central Utah who traveled through this area and may actually have seen the arch. It is difficult to photograph satisfactorily because of its secluded location. Hikers searching for the ideal viewpoint should be very careful on the surrounding slickrock; there is a sheer cliff just beyond the arch, and steep slickrock dips are treacherous.

This hike may be combined with the Frying Pan Trail (below) and Cohab Canyon Trail (above).

8 FRYING PAN TRAIL
(Strenuous)

Length one way - 3 miles between Cohab and Cassidy Arch trails, 5+ miles between parking areas, 6+ miles if combined with hike to Cassidy Arch

Trail may be entered from either end.

Parking areas - North: Campground at Fruita or Hickman Bridge parking area on U-24, South: end of road in Grand Wash

This delightful route takes the hiker along the summit of Capitol Reef, above and behind the west cliff face on one side, great Navajo domes and escarpments on the other. Rising about 800 feet, it is a strenuous trail with moderate slopes and ridges, sand and slickrock, canyons and flats, but climbing expertise is not required. Hikers with enough stamina may take side excursions cross-country to the west rim, or into the maze of rocky "breaks" along the route. (See Cohab and Cassidy Arch trails above.)

9 GOLDEN THRONE TRAIL

Length one way - 2 miles

(Fairly strenuous)   Parking area - in Capitol Gorge, 10.3 miles south of Visitor Center

For dramatic scenery, this trail ranks among the best in the park. It is a steep trail, climbing about 1,100 feet from the parking area to a flat near the base of Golden Throne, but not otherwise difficult.

Golden Throne, one of the highest points in the Reef, comes into view within the first half-mile and is a beacon thereafter. Actually one of several superb, golden-hued monoliths on the Reef's crest in this vicinity, the Throne stands out as a prominent landmark from Notom and other points to the east. The maintained trail ends at its base; beyond, to the north, prepared hikers may penetrate the extremely rugged territory between Capitol Gorge and Grand Wash. This is spectacular hiking terrain; overnight campers must register in advance with park personnel.

Views along the Golden Throne trail are superlative. To the south, Capitol Gorge flares out above its narrow inner chasm into a fantastic maze of rounded, sculptured rock forms, mostly in grand dimension, changing as a vision with the time of day and condition of sky. As in other places along the upper Reef, there is a seeming infinitude of shapes—of buttes and cones, fins and domes, cliffs, monuments, spires—all painted in delicate shades of white and cream, buff, red, tan, rust and gold. These exotic colors, together with the blue of the sky and green of the pygmy forest, create a natural kaleidoscope.

Peaks of the Henry Mountains rise to the east, the great swell of Miner's Mountain on the west.

10 FREMONT RIVER OVERLOOK TRAIL

Length one way - 1¼ mile

(Fairly strenuous)   Parking area - Main campground

A moderately strenuous hike, this trail includes an easy walk from the campground, through orchards and fields beside the Fremont River, then a steep climb up the slope of Miner's Mountain to an overlook point about 800 feet above the valley floor. This overlook affords a panoramic sweep along the face of Capitol Reef for many miles, as well as a thrilling view downward into Fruita Valley and Fremont River Canyon. There is also a high-level look at the majestic skyline of light-colored domes, cliffs and butte-forms that line the crest of Capitol Reef.

A voice is in the wind I do not know;
A meaning on the face of the high hills
Whose utterance I cannot comprehend.
A something is behind them: that is God.

MacDonald

Backcountry hiking *NPS photo*

Sulphur Creek Falls *NPS photo*

Narrows, Cohab Canyon *NPS photo*

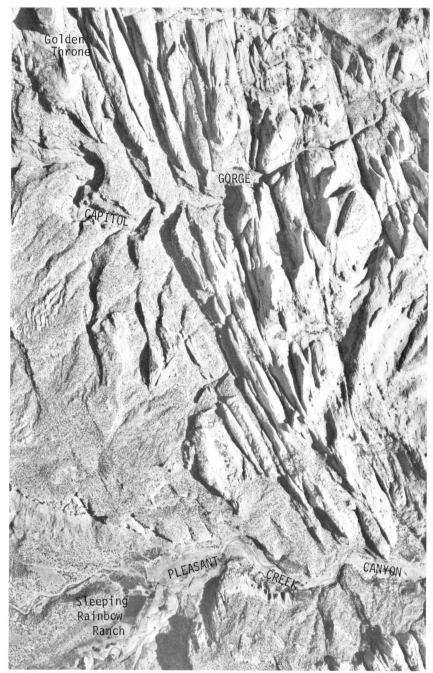

As seen from a high-flying survey aircraft: the incredibly rugged crest of the Water-pocket Fold between Golden Throne and Pleasant Creek Canyon. This is typical of back-country hiking and climbing terrain in the Capitol Reef section of the Fold. Maximum vertical relief: about 1,700 feet.

Department of Agriculture photo

BACKCOUNTRY HIKING

Most of Capitol Reef National Park remains in a wilderness state, not only because the general region is arid and sparsely populated but (more importantly) because the earth's surface here is so incredibly broken by uplift, fracturing and erosion that only hikers and climbers can penetrate it.

Except in the headquarters vicinity there are no marked or maintained trails. Most of the backcountry remains in its primitive and forbidding grandeur — almost untouched — beckoning the hardy, romantic and adventurous.

Because of the park's peculiar long and narrow shape, and the unusual nature of its terrain, it offers myriad choices to hikers, scramblers and climbers. The possible combinations seem to be endless, limited only by personal factors and the general necessity for carrying drinking water on whatever route one chooses.

Most backcountry hikers prefer canyon hiking, and there are scores of canyons in the park, ranging from short box canyons to 15-mile-long giants. Some are shallow and wide, most are very deep and narrow.

Combining canyon hiking with ridge scrambling and climbing can be exciting and rewarding. There is no practical limit to the opportunities for this type of activity, as the Waterpocket Fold is a literal labyrinth of rock erosion, hardly surpassed for intricacy.

A SPECIAL WORD OF CAUTION

Slickrock climbing and hiking can be safe and delightful — but potentially dangerous too, especially for the inexperienced. Slopes and dropoffs are deceptive: they can be easy to *descend*, but at the same time they may be difficult or impossible to *ascend* (if the way ahead is blocked). Use common sense...be cautious...keep out of trouble by looking behind as well as ahead!

For ease of description and reference, backcountry areas have been arranged here into three divisions: North, Central and South. No attempt has been made to describe routes in detail, other than special features or problems. Hikers will retain the incomparable pleasure of wilderness discovery for themselves.

Be sure to familiarize yourself with the list of *Safety Cautions, Regulations and Suggestions* at the end of this chapter. And always remember: it is best to consult with park rangers if in doubt about hiking conditions that may be encountered.

WATER

This is an arid land with only 5 to 7 inches of precipitation. Much of this comes as rain in late summer; there is comparatively little snow. There are springs, streams and waterpockets, if a person knows where to find them, but with hardly an exception these are not suited to human use without treatment. Backcountry hikers in Capitol Reef must provide their own water supply. In July and August, when daytime temperatures may exceed 100 degrees, a gallon of water per day is not too much for each hiker. In cooler months the quantity might be reduced somewhat — but it is always advisable to carry more water than you think you might need.

Double Arch *NPS photo*

NORTH DISTRICT BACKCOUNTRY
(Thousand Lake Mountain-South Desert-Cathedral Valley)

While long used by local stockmen for grazing, and penetrated by fairweather dirt roads, this area is sufficiently wild and rugged for most people.

Thousand Lake Mountain - South Desert

The Waterpocket Fold might be likened to a hundred-mile-long extension of Thousand Lake Mountain - an arm, so to speak, for its north end emerges from that lofty uplift. This northern end, most of which is within the park, is an awesome complex of deep canyons, great cliffs, vast areas of slickrock slopes, sand flats, and an assortment of grand erosional forms.

The outskirts of this rugged region may be reached by roads leading onto the mountain from Torrey (see page 51) and Fremont (see page 84). The former gives access to the upper reaches of Spring Canyon, as well as Water Canyon and Deep Creek via Paradise Flats. The latter is most convenient for direct access to upper Deep Creek and areas of the Fold north of Deep Creek, as well as the north end of South Desert and Cathedral Valley.

Backpackers have a choice of any number of challenging route combinations in this broken country. But there are few trails made by man (no park trails); hikers are on their own and must expect obstacles. *Carry a compass!* Orientation is difficult, even in an enclosed canyon.

Park rangers will be glad to make suggestions. Topographic maps, *indispensable for this area,* may offer clues. Or local ranchers might give useful hints.

Two routes in particular might appeal to hardy backpackers desiring longer hikes in very rugged, secluded wilderness. Caution: It is recommended that hikers not hike alone in this country — especially those not familiar with the terrain.

1. **DEEP CREEK** begins in Deep Creek Lake, under the mountain's rim at 10,500 feet, and empties into South Desert about 15 trail miles away. Its water has been diverted near the upper end, so the creekbed is dry for the most part. For much of its length the creekbed is enclosed between beautifully sculptured walls up to 600 feet high or more, these walls becoming more variegated in color toward the east. Large rock falls and lack of water in the canyon's lower end make this a difficult hike. Expect the unexpected.

Hikers can reach the canyon's upper end by walking several miles from Elkhorn Ranger Station or the Polk Creek (Cathedral Valley) road.

Water Canyon is a very scenic tributary of Deep Creek. Able

Vicinity of Deep Creek-Water Canyon confluence. Deep Creek is at lower right; Water Canyon, upper left. This picture illustrates hiking terrain in the northern part of Water-pocket Fold. Water Canyon is about 700 feet deep here. *NPS photo.*

hikers with time to explore might find a way down into its precipitous upper end (reached from Torrey); otherwise, its more spectacular lower reaches can be entered from Deep Creek. There is water in this canyon about 2 miles upstream from Deep Creek.

After reaching South Desert, a very scenic valley between the slopes of Waterpocket Fold on the west and a line of cliffs to the east, hikers must then continue to a road where they can be picked up. The closest vehicle roads are those giving access to Cathedral Valley.

Choice 1: Hike through South Desert along an abandoned road to the north end of the valley and ascend switchbacks to the top of a ridge. This will bring hikers to the Cathedral Valley road at Mile 24, Road Log No. 5. Distance about 7 miles.

Choice 2: Cross South Desert in a south easterly direction, bearing toward the group of cathedral buttes and break in the eastern cliff that mark Lower South Desert Overlook (mile 12, Road Log No. 5). The southern end of the abandoned road mentioned above leads to this overlook. Distance: 4 to 5 miles.

Choice 3: Continue from Deep Creek Canyon south along the length of South Desert to Fremont River and Highway U-24, a distance of about 11 miles. This route, while longer, avoids the necessity of the pickup vehicle having to travel for many mile on rough dirt roads. *No drinking water available on any of these alternatives!*

Depending on points of entrance and exit, the Deep Creek hike would total from 20 to 26 miles and would require from 2 to 3 days. Mountain access roads are normally closed from November to early May; plan accordingly.

This hike offers advantages of variegated scenery (mountain, enclosed red-rock canyon, open desert valley) and downward-to-level grade. But water must be carried.

2. **SPRING CANYON** is the park's longest and largest canyon, beginning on the slopes of Thousand Lake Mountain at more than 8,000 feet. From there it follows an unusually direct course for much of its nearly 15-mile length, descending about 3,000 feet before joining Fremont River Canyon and Highway U-24 at a point 3.7 miles east of the Visitor Center. Its upper end, an abrupt dropoff, can be surveyed from the Torrey forest road (see page 51). A feasible route into the upper canyon is a stock trail leading through the "W" notch north of Rimrock Motel. Or hikers can hike up-canyon from Chimney Rock Canyon.

Spring Canyon is 400 to 600 feet deep and rather open through much of its length. It has been used for stock grazing and there is water in places. A spring is located 1½ miles up-canyon from Chimney Rock Canyon; this can be used for drinking (but treat!). In its upper reaches the canyon is cut into the colorful formations of Capitol Reef's face; farther down its walls are formed by massive, gently contoured Navajo sandstone, and here it becomes a labyrinth of marvelous erosional forms.

The entire Spring Canyon route offers a pleasant 2-day challenge for backpackers willing to carry a supply of water. A shorter alternative is the following:

3. **Chimney Rock-lower Spring Canyon Route** between Chimney Rock Trail parking area on Highway U-24 (see page 90 of this chapter) and the mouth of Spring Canyon. Chimney Rock Canyon joins Spring Canyon about 6½ miles from the latter's mouth, 2½ miles from the Chimney Rock trailhead near U-24, making a total hiking distance of about 9 miles. This is an exceptionally scenic route that may be hiked in one day of 6 hours, or more leisurely in two. The route ends in Fremont River Canyon at the highway, mile 3.7 of Road Log No. 3. Carry drinking water.

Cathedral Valley Area

Much of the Cathedral Valley area is visible from the road. However, there are numerous pockets, amphitheaters and secluded draws that are inaccessible to wheeled vehicles. Many of these are scenically exciting for those desiring short exploratory hikes of a few hours, or even a day or more. Such rugged and remote areas as The Hartnet, Black Mountain, Wood Bench, and the breaks of Caineville Wash are not far from the access road, yet they offer the challenge and adventure of exploring a little known country on foot.

CENTRAL DISTRICT BACKCOUNTRY

Consisting as it does of the park's best-known core—formerly Capitol Reef National Monument—the Central District has been developed with a number of marked and maintained trails, as described in Part 1 of this chapter.

Backpackers and off-trail hikers, however, often use these trails as access routes for exploring the Reef's myriad side canyons and slickrock maze (sometimes called the "rock jungle"). As shown by aerial photographs, this part of the Waterpocket Fold truly is a tangle of crisscrossing gorges, fins, domes and ridges. What is not apparent in photos is the actual three-dimensional *scale* of these physical features—a precipitous scale measured in hundreds of feet.

In other words, for those desiring to get away from it all, without driving too far from the paved highway, the maintained trails described in Part 1 are portals for off-trail personal exploration.

Several possibilities include the following (inquire and register at the Visitor Center or with rangers before attempting these routes):

— Rim hiking between Cohab Canyon and Grand Wash
— Exploring the summit "breaks" between Grand Wash and Capitol Gorge
— Exploring the incredibly rugged high country between Capitol Gorge and Pleasant Creek Canyon

Fremont River Canyon

Many people have hiked through Fremont River Canyon between the Torrey-Grover highway and Fruita. This 9-mile hike requires some stream wading (up to a foot or two of water), but it passes through a spectacular 1,000-foot-deep gorge and is scenically outstanding. It can be done in one day, but two days would be more enjoyable. Carry drinking water, or purify the river water before using.

Sulphur Creek Canyon

Others have hiked through the deep, narrow, winding gorge of Sulphur Creek. The gorge can be entered from Highway U-24 where it crosses Sulphur Creek (mile 6.9, Road Log No. 2), or even closer to Fruita by way of several tributary canyons visible from the highway. The longest hiking distance would be only 6 or 7 miles and could easily be traversed in a day. Carry drinking water. Expect shoe wetting; shallow wading might be necessary.

There are other backcountry hiking possibilities in the Central District. Park personnel will be glad to make suggestions. Mention might be made of Miner's Mountain, the great rounded swell between Capitol Reef and Boulder Mountain. Short hikes up the slopes of Miner's Mountain, taken from points along the South Reef Drive, are very rewarding in the way of dramatic panoramic views of the Reef's rainbow face.

SOUTH DISTRICT BACKCOUNTRY
(Southern Waterpocket Fold)

The South District is most easily accessible from the Notom-Burr Trail-Bullfrog Marina road that follows along the Fold's eastern slope. Many of this area's hiking possibilities are coordinated with that road in Road Log No. 4. Inasmuch as the shorter hiking routes are described there, hikers interested in the South District must refer to that log as well as to the descriptions of longer routes appearing below. Short routes described in Road Log No. 4 are the following:

Mileage reading in log	Hiking area
6.4	Slickrock slopes between Pleasant Creek Canyon and Capitol Gorge
8.1	Burro Wash
	Cottonwood Wash
	Fivemile Wash
15.0	North and South Coleman Canyons
22.2	Red Canyon
33.9	Canyon breaks near Burr Trail and The Post
35.8	Surprise Canyon
36.3	The Post. Parking area for Halls Creek (Grand Gulch) and Lower Muley Twist hikers
46.7	Brimhall Natural Bridge; Lower Halls Creek (Grand Gulch)
37.0 (west fork)	Strike Valley Overlook

Certain backcountry hiking routes in the South District might also be approached from the west—from the Boulder Mountain road (Road Log No. 2), the Tantalus Flats road, and even the Circle Cliffs road. This applies in particular to Sheets Gulch and Oak Creek Canyon. However, since access conditions on the west may change from time to time—depending on weather, season, road conditions, etc.—they are not described in detail here. Interested parties should consult with park rangers about the most feasible routes for approaching canyons of the Fold from the west.

(1) **Pleasant Creek Canyon** cuts through the Fold between Sleeping Rainbow (Floral) Ranch on the west and Notom on the east. Pleasant Creek is a perennial stream and potable with treatment; it is advisable, however, to carry drinking water.

The canyon is exceptionally scenic, about 3 miles long through the Reef, with walls rising hundreds of feet on either side. Exiting from the Reef, Pleasant Creek flows another 3 miles through relatively open country to Notom, a total distance of about 6 miles. However, there is a shorter cutoff from the mouth of the canyon to a road leading from Notom Bench (see mile 6.4, Road Log No. 4); this alternative requires a one-way hike of only 3 or 4 miles.

Hikers not wishing to arrange for pickup may prefer to walk a mile or two into the most scenic part of the canyon from either direction—the ranch on the west, the Notom road on the east—then return to their cars. Those hiking from the west may park in the valley below Sleeping Rainbow Guest Ranch (private), which sits on a ridge to the north. No camping facilities here; observe park regulations.

Those approaching from the east may turn off the main road at mile 6.4 (Road Log No. 4) and drive a short distance west to the park boundary. From that point it is only 3 or 4 miles completely through the canyon to the ranch.

(2) **Sheets Gulch** is one of the more spectacular canyons in the park, and its grandeur can best be appreciated by hikers. The Gulch's eastern end is accessible from the Waterpocket Fold road (see mile 13.3, Road Log No. 4). Hikers may leave their cars there and hike several miles into its narrows. However, a dropoff of about 8 feet in the narrows makes through-travel from east to west a problem unless a log, for example, can be found to surmount this obstacle. In the other direction, ropes can be used. The canyon is fairly open for the most part and is grandly scenic. Carry water.

The canyon's west end can be reached from the Tantalus Flats road; inquire about details from park rangers.

(3) **Oak Creek Canyon** is only about 2 miles long where it cuts through the Fold in a deep, narrow gorge. However, in its higher reaches west of this gorge, the canyon is notable for the beauty and grandeur of its walls, which rise almost sheer for 600 to 800 feet. They do not close in here as they do through the Fold, but are as much as a mile apart—an effect of spacious depth that is not usual among the park's canyons.

Hikers going from west to east find that Oak Creek provides a delightful downhill walking experience. There is clear water all year (drinkable after treatment), luxuriant streamside vegetation, and the coolness of high country—pleasant attributes lacking in much of this area. Even in the canyon's lower reaches there are water and vegetation.

Depending on road conditions on the west, the hiking route may vary in length up to 15 miles (one way, through the canyon). The ideal would be for west-to-east hikers to plan a 2-day backpacking excursion from the vicinity of Lower Bown's Reservoir on Boulder Mountain, meeting their pickup vehicle at the mouth of the canyon near Sandy Junction.

Hikers approaching from the east on the Waterpocket Fold road (see mile 14.4, Road Log No. 4) can park their vehicles at the ford and hike upstream as far as they like. The canyon is popular for both overnight and day hikes. Purify the stream water before drinking, or carry your own.

(4) **Upper and Lower Muley Twist Canyons,** at the upper end of Burr Trail, are two of the park's outstanding backcountry hiking routes.

(a). **Lower Muley Twist Canyon.** Parking area and hiking register, 2 miles west of Burr Junction (mile 33.9, Road Log No. 4). A remarkable gorge that has been cut into the crest of the Waterpocket Fold, parallel to the Fold's north-south direction, the canyon winds tortuously for 12 miles before exiting into Halls Creek Canyon (Grand Gulch). Light-colored Navajo sandstone of the Fold's slope-face forms Muley Twist's eastern wall; layered Kayenta and fractured red Wingate sandstone are its floor and west wall.

Remaining much as it was when first used as a travel route a hundred years ago, before Burr Trail was built, Lower Muley Twist is a hiker's favorite. It is valued for a rare atmosphere of wildness and cloistered solitude, where the hiker is surrounded by the unique beauty and wonder of canyon country.

Walls and slopes close in, or overhang, or spread apart in places. Always there is the awesome spectacle of infinite variety in form and design in rock: cliff faces sculptured in patterns never conceived by human brain; gargoyles, standing rocks, domes, spires—erosional forms that defy classification or naming.

Hikers may choose to hike the entire 12 miles to Halls Creek. In this event it is another 5 miles by trail to the nearest parking area (The Post). If arrangements have not been made for auto pickup there, it is an additional 4 miles or so from The Post to parking area at trailhead atop the Burr Trail. At least two days should be allowed for this hike, which can total more than 20 miles. *Carry sufficient water.*

An alternative choice is to hike Muley Twist for only the first 4 miles, then exit via the Cutoff Trail to The Post (2½ miles). From The Post it is slightly more than 4 miles back to trailhead parking. This may be an easy one-day hike of 6½ miles, or a longer hike of 11 miles, depending on whether the hiker arranges vehicle pickup at The Post.

(b). **Upper Muley Twist Canyon.** Junction with Circle Cliffs road, 3.1 miles west of Burr Junction (mile 33.9, Road Log No. 4). 4-wheel-drive vehicles may be driven along Upper Muley Twist Canyon from junction for a distance of 2.9 miles; road ends at a parking area. A short hike to the east brings one to the Strike Valley Overlook, described in Road Log No. 4.

Straight ahead from the parking area, Upper Muley Twist Canyon continues northward along the Fold's crest for another 6½ miles. The canyon is exceptionally scenic, having an abundance of vivid colors and curious erosional designs so characteristic of the area's rocks.

There are natural arches along the trail, one of them known as Saddle Arch but most remaining unnamed. About 5 miles from the parking area, hikers can decide whether to continue to the end of the canyon, or retrace the route they came, or make a circle return via the

"The Backbone," Sheets Gulch area   *NPS photo*

Rim Route trail. This latter affords dramatic vistas in all directions.

Another alternative is to climb out of the basin at the upper end of the canyon, turn east and descend the slope of the Fold to Bitter Creek Divide (mile 25.8, Road Log No. 4). This would necessitate pickup at the divide, as it is 14 miles by road from there to the parking area (trailhead) in Upper Muley Twist Canyon.

(5) **Halls Creek (Grand Gulch)** offers wilderness hiking and exploring in remote red-rock country. Extending for about 30 miles south of Burr Trail to Lake Powell in Glen Canyon, this backcountry route passes along the floor of a deep valley between the massive sandstone slope of Waterpocket Fold on the west, a precipitous cliff on the east.

There are exploring opportunities enough in this strange land of narrow box canyons and convoluted slopes to occupy an energetic and curious hiker for days or even weeks. And there is water in springs and pockets during much of the year. But this water may not be potable even if it can be found, and therefore hikers not familiar with the area are advised to carry all the drinking water they expect to need. This requirement, of course, is a serious limitation on the length of time that can be spent in the area.

Additional information about Halls Creek can be found in Road Log No. 4. Hikers interested in this area should consult with park rangers.

FOR HIKERS
CAUTIONS, REGULATIONS and SUGGESTIONS

General
- Hiking is most pleasant during spring and fall. Summers are hot, winters cold.
- Do not enter narrow streambeds during stormy or threatening weather. Dangerous floods may come from far away. If caught in heavy rain, move to high ground immediately.
- Carry sufficient drinking water. Wear suitable shoes and clothing, including a hat. Insect repellent and suntan lotion may be desirable. Take along extra film (more than you plan to use).
- Hike in pairs or groups if possible.
- Possession, destruction or removal of any native animals, plants, rock samples or artifacts is prohibited within the park.
- Do not gather or cut any native wood for a fire. Fires are restricted to established fireplaces.
- Pets are not allowed on trails or more than 100 yards from roads.
- Try hiking in the evening with a flashlight. It can be a delightful experience!

Maintained trails
- Keep to the trail. Do not shortcut. Do not throw or roll rocks.
- Camping is not permitted within ½ mile of any trail, except at an established campsite.
- Carry drinking water if you expect to hike more than an hour or so. A pint of water per person per hour should be sufficient under ordinary conditions.

Backcountry hiking and backpacking
- Be prepared! Anticipate unusual situations and prepare for them in advance. Become acquainted with your proposed route by talking with rangers or others who are familiar with it. Carry topographic maps.
- Travel with a companion if possible. If not, advise someone else of your route and schedule. All overnight backcountry hikers must fill out a use permit in advance at the Visitor Center.
- Carry a first aid kit and know how to use it. Know the symptoms and treatment for heat stroke and heat exhaustion. In winter, know how to recognize and treat hypothermia.
- Carry sufficient water if you are not certain that local water is available. In most areas of the park it is not. Local water should be treated or boiled before drinking. During summer months at least 1 or 2 gallons of water per person per day is necessary for survival. Rocks become very hot, and they store heat!
- Carry adequate provisions and equipment. Wear a hat. Remember

that nights are cool, even in summer; prepare accordingly. Biting and stinging insects can be bothersome in any part of the park during warmer months; wear long sleeves and/or carry repellent if this may be a problem for you.

- Do not camp in streambeds; floods can occur at night. Pack out everything that you carry in. Never bury trash. Use a backpacking stove; do not burn available wood in the park.
- Practice "low impact" hiking and camping. Leave the environment as pristine as you found it. Those who follow will be grateful.

MAP INFORMATION

At this writing, no detailed general-purpose map is devoted especially to Capitol Reef National Park. However, the park is included in a number of maps covering larger and smaller areas: for example, various topographic maps of the U.S. Geological Survey.

The park is shown in fair detail, also, on highway maps, geological maps, multipurpose maps, mineral maps, etc. Those of most value to sightseers and hikers are listed below:

U.S. Geological Survey

Topographic contour maps (quadrangle maps)
15 minute series, scale 1:62,500
Those covering the park area are shown on the accompanying diagram
Large scale contour maps, scale 1:250,000
- Salina quadrangle (includes north half of park)
- Escalante quadrangle (includes south half of park)

Geologic maps
- Geology, Structure and Uranium Deposits of the Salina Quadrangle, Utah. Misc. Geol. Investigations Map I-591. USGS 1971.
- Geology, Structure and Uranium Deposits of the Escalante Quadrangle, Utah-Arizona. Misc. Geol. Investigations Map I-744. USGS 1973.

Availability of USGS maps:

Order by mail from Distribution Section, USGS, Silver Spring, MD. 20910 or Distribution Section, USGS, Denver Federal Center, Denver, CO. 80225

Over-the-counter:

USGS Public Inquiries Office, 125 S. State, Salt Lake City, UT 84111

Park Visitor Center: Those maps shown on accompanying diagram are usually available for purchase at the Visitor Center.

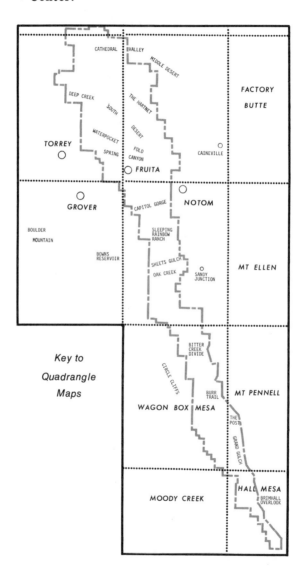

Utah Travel Council (address Council Hall, Salt Lake City, UT 84114)

Utah Multipurpose Maps (showing highways, points of interest, contours, etc.) Scale 1:250,000. There is a charge for these maps.

- No. 1 Southeastern Utah (includes most of the park south of North District)
- No. 2 Southeastern-Central Utah (includes North District of park, north of Highway 24)

GENERAL PARK REGULATIONS

(see page 108 for Hiking Regulations, Cautions and Suggestions)

1. Hunting, trapping or use of firearms is prohibited. Firearms must be unloaded and cased or broken down.
2. All vehicles, including motorbikes, must remain on maintained roads or in designated parking areas.
3. Overnight camping should be in designated areas.
4. Backpackers should contact a ranger or Visitor Center to obtain backcountry camping permits before taking any overnight trips.
5. Build fires only in established fireplaces. Fuel-burning stoves must be used in the backcountry. Do not gather or cut any native wood for a fire.
6. Possession, destruction or removal of any native animals, plants, rock samples or artifacts is prohibited.
7. Pets are not allowed on trails or more than 100 yards from roads. Pets must be kept on a leash or under physical control at all times.
8. Do not litter! Please carry out what you carry in.

FACILITIES, SERVICES AND SUPPLIES

Within the park — No commercial facilities or services other than limited film supply and publications at Visitor Center.

Campground with tables, restrooms, water, charcoal firestands. Fee area. First-come, first-served basis. No trailer hookups. Nearly always filled by early afternoon in summer months.

Picnic areas.

Commercial accommodations, facilities and services are located outside the park on Highway U-24 —

8 miles west - Rimrock Motel/Restaurant/Trailer Park

11 miles west - Torrey (store, motel, service stations, restaurant, trailer parking)

14 to 27 miles west - Upper valley towns (stores, motels, restaurants, service stations, trailer parking, garages)

19 miles east - Caineville (restaurant, limited supplies)

39 miles east - Hanksville (restaurants, stores, service stations, garages, motels, trailer parking)

SUGGESTED READING

Description and History (Canyonlands Region in general)

Abbey, Edward. *Desert Solitaire: A Season in the Wilderness.* 1968.

Abbey, Edward and Philip Hyde. *Slickrock: The Canyon Country of Southeast Utah.* 1971.

Crampton, C. Gregory. *Standing Up Country: The Canyon Lands of Utah and Arizona.* 1964.

Stegner, Wallace. *Beyond the Hundredth Meridian: John Wesley Powell and the Second Opening of the West.* 1954.

Description and History (Capitol Reef)

Olson, Virgil and David Muench. *Capitol Reef: The Story Behind the Scenery.* 1972.

Trimble, Stephen. *Rock Glow, Sky Shine: The Spirit of Capitol Reef.* 1978. Published by Capitol Reef Natural History Association.

Indians

Gunnerson, James H. *The Fremont Culture: A Study in Culture Dynamics on the Northern Anasazi Frontier.* Papers of the Peabody Museum, Vol. 59, 1969.

Schaafsma, Polly. *The Rock Art of Utah.* Papers of the Peabody Museum, Vol. 65, 1971.

Biology

Elsmore, F. H. and J. R. Janish. *Shrubs and Trees of the Southwest Uplands.* 1976.

Jaeger, Edmund C. *Desert Wildlife.* 1961 +.

Geology

Hunt, Charles B. et al. *Geology and Geography of the Henry Mountains Region, Utah.* U.S. Geological Survey Professional Paper No. 228. 1953.

Smith, J. Fred, et al. *Geology of the Capitol Reef Area.* U.S. Geological Survey Professional Paper No. 363. 1963.

Many of the publications listed above are available from the Capitol Reef Natural History Association, Capitol Reef National Park, Torrey, Utah 84775.

Eph Hanks "had found the most beautiful country that God ever made... in a fierce, primitive way that stole your breath and made your head light."

Sidney A. Hanks (his son)